UTMOST

UTMOST

CLASSIC READINGS AND PRAYERS

from

⁓ *My Utmost for His Highest* ⁓

OSWALD CHAMBERS

Discovery House.
from Our Daily Bread Ministries

United States publication rights are held by Discovery House, which is affiliated with Our Daily Bread Ministries, Grand Rapids, Michigan.

Unless otherwise indicated, Scripture quotations are from The New King James Version. Copyright © 1979, 1980, 1982 by Thomas Nelson, Inc., Publishers. Used by permission.

Requests for permission to quote from this book should be directed to: Permissions Department, Discovery House, P.O. Box 3566, Grand Rapids, MI 49501 or contact us by e-mail at permissionsdept@dhp.org

Interior design by Sherri L. Hoffman

ISBN 978-1-57293-569-3

Printed in the United States of America

Third printing in 2015

⌒ INTRODUCTION ⌒

For over eighty years Oswald Chambers' *My Utmost for His Highest* has been one of the most widely read books in the Christian world. First published in England in 1927, and in the United States in 1935, these daily readings were compiled from shorthand notes of Chambers' lectures and talks by his wife, "Biddy," who was a professional stenographer.

Through the years, countless people from various walks of life and from diverse backgrounds have been influenced by this classic devotional work. Now we are pleased to release this special edition of ninety devotionals selected from *My Utmost for His Highest*, designed to introduce a new generation to the timeless truths of Scripture as taught through the enduring words of Oswald Chambers. These selections also include Oswald Chambers' personal prayers with each devotional.

⇜ A WORD ABOUT ⇝
Oswald Chambers

Oswald Chambers was born in Aberdeen, Scotland, on July 24, 1874. When he was fifteen, the family moved to London where Oswald made his public profession of faith in Christ and became a member of Rye Lane Baptist Church. This marked a period of rapid spiritual growth, along with an intense struggle to find God's will and way for his life.

While studying at the University of Edinburgh (1895–96), he experienced a major redirection in life and decided to train for the Christian ministry. He left the university and entered Dunoon College, near Glasgow, where he spent nine years, first as a theological student, then as a tutor of philosophy. Under the wise guidance of Rev. Duncan MacGregor, his mentor and friend, Oswald matured greatly and came through a long "dark night of the soul" into a deeper and more joyful knowledge of Christ.

In 1906 and 1907 Oswald spent six months teaching at God's Bible School in Cincinnati, Ohio. From there he went to Japan, visiting the Tokyo Bible School, founded by Charles and Lettie Cowman. While serving as a traveling speaker and representative of the League of Prayer in Britain, Oswald met Gertrude Hobbs. Their friendship blossomed during a voyage to the United States in the summer of 1908, and two years later they were married. Oswald called her "Beloved Disciple," shortened to the initials B.D., and spoken as "Biddy." For the rest of her life, she was known by this affectionate nickname. Their only child, Kathleen, was born in May 1913.

A longtime dream of Oswald's became reality in January 1911 with the opening of the Bible Training College (BTC) near Clapham Common in London, where he served as Principal and main teacher. During Oswald's lectures Biddy sat in the back of the room recording his words verbatim in her precise Pittman's shorthand. Trained as a court stenographer, she could take dictation rapidly while remaining engaged with her husband's purpose as he taught.

The outbreak of World War I in August 1914 led to the closing of the BTC within a year. Oswald volunteered as a YMCA secretary in Egypt, where Biddy, Kathleen, and several former students from the BTC joined him to assist in the work. At Zeitoun Camp, near Cairo, Oswald quickly established himself as a friend of the troops and a man of uncommon spiritual insight.

In late October 1917 Oswald underwent an emergency appendectomy and appeared to be recovering. But two weeks later, while still in hospital, he suffered a relapse and died early in the morning on November 15. He was forty-three years old.

For the next two years, Biddy and Kathleen continued to work among the troops at Zeitoun. Gradually it became clear to Biddy that her calling in life was to give her husband's words to the world. In so doing, she continued the dream she and Oswald had shared of working together to help others. Upon her return to England in 1919, Biddy continued transcribing her shorthand notes and preparing them for publication.

While maintaining a boarding house for students in Oxford, Biddy compiled a book of daily readings which she titled *My Utmost for His Highest*. Since it was first published in 1927, *My Utmost* has been continuously in print and has sold millions of copies. It exists today in more than forty different languages, and every day, multiplied thousands of people around the world open its pages seeking a word from the Lord through His servant Oswald Chambers.

—DAVID McCASLAND

ᵔ UTMOST ᵔ

⌒ DAY 1 ⌒

Let Us Keep to the Point

". . . my earnest expectation and hope that in nothing I shall be ashamed, but with all boldness, as always, so now also Christ will be magnified in my body, whether by life or by death."

—PHILIPPIANS 1:20

My **Utmost for His Highest.** ". . . my earnest expectation and hope that in nothing I shall be ashamed . . . ." We will all feel very much ashamed if we do not yield to Jesus the areas of our lives He has asked us to yield to Him. It's as if Paul were saying, "My determined purpose is to be my utmost for His highest—my best for His glory." To reach that level of determination is a matter of the will, not of debate or of reasoning. It is absolute and irrevocable surrender of the will at that point. An undue amount of thought and consideration for ourselves is what keeps us from making that decision, although we cover it up with the pretense that it is others we are considering. When we think seriously about what it will cost others if we obey the call of Jesus, we tell God He doesn't know what our obedience will mean. Keep to the point—He does know. Shut out every other thought and keep yourself before God in this one thing only—my utmost for His highest. I am determined to be absolutely and entirely for Him and Him alone.

My Unstoppable Determination for His Holiness. "Whether it means life or death—it makes no difference!" (see 1:21). Paul was determined that nothing would stop him from doing exactly what God wanted. But before we choose to follow God's will, a crisis must develop in our lives. This happens because we tend to be unresponsive to God's gentler nudges. He brings us to the place where He asks us to be our utmost for Him and we begin to debate. He then providentially produces a crisis where we have to decide—for or against. That moment becomes a great crossroads in our lives. If a crisis has come to you on any front, surrender your will to Jesus absolutely and irrevocably.

Lord, the range of Your power, the touch of Your grace, the breathing of Your Spirit—how I long for these to bring me face to face with You. Forgive my tardiness; it takes me so long to awaken to some things.

☞ DAY 2 ☜

The Voice of the Nature of God

"I heard the voice of the Lord, saying: 'Whom shall I send, and who will go for Us?'" —ISAIAH 6:8

When we talk about the call of God, we often forget the most important thing, namely, the nature of Him who calls. There are many things calling each of us today. Some of these calls will be answered, and others will not even be heard. The call is the expression of the nature of the One who calls, and we can only recognize the call if that same nature is in us. The call of God is the expression of God's nature, not ours. God providentially weaves the threads of His call through our lives, and only we can distinguish them. It is the threading of God's voice directly to us over a certain concern, and it is useless to seek another person's opinion of it. Our dealings over the call of God should be kept exclusively between ourselves and Him.

The call of God is not a reflection of my nature; my personal desires and temperament are of no consideration. As long as I dwell on my own qualities and traits and think about what I am suited for, I will never hear the call of God. But when God brings me into the right relationship with Himself, I will be in the same condition Isaiah was. Isaiah was so attuned to God, because of the great crisis he had just endured, that the call of God penetrated his soul. The majority of us cannot hear anything but ourselves. And we cannot hear anything God says. But to be brought to the place where we can hear the call of God is to be profoundly changed.

"Let me hear Your voice"—that is my prayer. I am willing beyond all my expression to hear You, to perceive You, to be thrilled with Your presence.

⌒ DAY 3 ⌒
The Call of the Natural Life

"When it pleased God . . . to reveal His Son in me . . . ."
—GALATIANS 1:15–16

The call of God is not a call to serve Him in any particular way. My contact with the nature of God will shape my understanding of His call and will help me realize what I truly desire to do for Him. The call of God is an expression of His nature; the service which results in my life is suited to me and is an expression of my nature. The call of the natural life was stated by the apostle Paul—"When it pleased God . . . to reveal His Son in me, that I might *preach* Him [that is, *purely and solemnly express* Him] among the Gentiles . . . ."

Service is the overflow which pours from a life filled with love and devotion. But strictly speaking, there is no *call* to that. Service is what I bring to the relationship and is the reflection of my identification with the nature of God. Service becomes a natural part of my life. God brings me into the proper relationship with Himself so that I can understand His call, and then I serve Him on my own out of a motivation of absolute love. Service to God is the deliberate love-gift of a nature that has heard the call of God. Service is an expression of my nature, and God's call is an expression of His nature. Therefore, when I receive His nature and hear His call, His divine voice resounds throughout His nature and mine and the two become one in service. The Son of God reveals Himself in me, and out of devotion to Him service becomes my everyday way of life.

Lord, Your Word comes so quietly and all-pervadingly—"If any man serve Me, let him follow Me," and, "If any man serve Me, him will my Father honor." Take me as Your servant in this sense.

∽ DAY 4 ∽

"It Is the Lord!"

"Thomas answered and said to Him, 'My Lord and my God!'"
—JOHN 20:28

Jesus said to her, 'Give Me a drink'" (John 4:7). How many of us are expecting Jesus Christ to quench our thirst when we should be satisfying Him! We should be pouring out our lives, investing our total beings, not drawing on Him to satisfy us. "You shall be witnesses to Me . . ." (Acts 1:8). That means lives of pure, uncompromising, and unrestrained devotion to the Lord Jesus, which will be satisfying to Him wherever He may send us.

Beware of anything that competes with your loyalty to Jesus Christ. The greatest competitor of true devotion to Jesus is the service we do for Him. It is easier to serve than to pour out our lives completely for Him. The goal of the call of God is His satisfaction, not simply that we should do something *for* Him. We are not sent to do battle for God, but to be used by God in His battles. Are we more devoted to service than we are to Jesus Christ Himself?

———————

I praise You for that word—"Like as a father pitieth his children, so the Lord pitieth them that fear Him." How I realize that I owe nothing to Your severity but all to Your love. Oh, that Your Love and gentleness and patience toward me were expressed through me to others!

⌐ DAY 5 ⌐

Vision and Darkness

"When the sun was going down, a deep sleep fell upon Abram; and behold, horror and great darkness fell upon him."

—GENESIS 15:12

Whenever God gives a vision to a Christian, it is as if He puts him in "the shadow of His hand" (Isaiah 49:2). The saint's duty is to be still and listen. There is a "darkness" that comes from too much light—that is the time to listen. The story of Abram and Hagar in Genesis 16 is an excellent example of listening to so-called good advice during a time of darkness, rather than waiting for God to send the light. When God gives you a vision and darkness follows, wait. God will bring the vision He has given you to reality in your life if you will wait on His timing. Never try to help God fulfill His word. Abram went through thirteen years of silence, but in those years all of his self-sufficiency was destroyed. He grew past the point of relying on his own common sense. Those years of silence were a time of discipline, not a period of God's displeasure. There is never any need to pretend that your life is filled with joy and confidence; just wait upon God and be grounded in Him (see Isaiah 50:10–11).

Do I trust at all in the flesh? Or have I learned to go beyond all confidence in myself and other people of God? Do I trust in books and prayers or other joys in my life? Or have I placed my confidence in God *Himself*, not in His blessings? "I am Almighty God . . ." —El-Shaddai, the All-Powerful God (Genesis 17:1). The reason we are all being disciplined is that we will know God is real. As soon as God becomes real to us, people pale by comparison, becoming shadows of reality. Nothing that other saints do or say can ever upset the one who is built on God.

O Lord, with much dimness I draw nigh to You. Clear the dimness away from me and flood me with the light of Your countenance.

Are You Fresh for Everything?

"Jesus answered and said to him, 'Most assuredly, I say to you, unless one is born again, he cannot see the kingdom of God.'" —JOHN 3:3

Sometimes we are fresh and eager to attend a prayer meeting, but do we feel that same freshness for such mundane tasks as polishing shoes?

Being born again by the Spirit is an unmistakable work of God, as mysterious as the wind, and as surprising as God Himself. We don't know where it begins—it is hidden away in the depths of our soul. Being born again from above is an enduring, perpetual, and eternal beginning. It provides a freshness all the time in thinking, talking, and living—a continual surprise of the life of God. Staleness is an indication that something in our lives is out of step with God. We say to ourselves, "I have to do this thing or it will never get done." That is the first sign of staleness. Do we feel fresh this very moment or are we stale, frantically searching our minds for something to do? Freshness is not the result of obedience; it comes from the Holy Spirit. Obedience keeps us "in the light as He is in the light . . ." (1 John 1:7).

Jealously guard your relationship with God. Jesus prayed "that they may be one just as We are one"—with nothing in between (John 17:22). Keep your whole life continually open to Jesus Christ. Don't pretend to be open with Him. Are you drawing your life from any source other than God Himself? If you are depending on something else as your source of freshness and strength, you will not realize when His power is gone.

Being born of the Spirit means much more than we usually think. It gives us new vision and keeps us absolutely fresh for everything through the never-ending supply of the life of God.

O Lord, breathe on me till I am one with You in the temper of my mind and heart and disposition. Unto You do I turn. Again, how completely I realize my lostness without You!

❧ DAY 7 ❧

Recall What God Remembers

"Thus says the Lord: 'I remember . . . the kindness of your youth . . . .'"
—JEREMIAH 2:2

Am I as spontaneously kind to God as I used to be, or am I only expecting God to be kind to me?

Does everything in my life fill His heart with gladness, or do I constantly complain because things don't seem to be going my way? A person who has forgotten what God treasures will not be filled with joy. It is wonderful to remember that Jesus Christ has needs which we can meet—"Give Me a drink" (John 4:7). How much kindness have I shown Him in the past week? Has my life been a good reflection on His reputation?

God is saying to His people, "You are not in love with Me now, but I remember a time when you were." He says, "I remember . . . the love of your betrothal . . ." (Jeremiah 2:2). Am I as filled to overflowing with love for Jesus Christ as I was in the beginning, when I went out of my way to prove my devotion to Him? Does He ever find me pondering the time when I cared only for Him? Is that where I am now, or have I chosen man's wisdom over true love for Him? Am I so in love with Him that I take no thought for where He might lead me? Or am I watching to see how much respect I get as I measure how much service I should give Him?

As I recall what God remembers about me, I may also begin to realize that He is not what He used to be to me. When this happens, I should allow the shame and humiliation it creates in my life, because it will bring godly sorrow, and "godly sorrow produces repentance . . ." (2 Corinthians 7:10).

———

Lord, how I long for You to bring me face to face with Yourself! My soul thirsts for You, for the touch of Your grace, the breathing of Your Spirit.

⌒ DAY 8 ⌒

Am I Looking to God?

"Look to Me, and be saved . . . ."　　　　　　　　—ISAIAH 45:22

Do we expect God to come to us with His blessings and save us? He says, *"Look to Me*, and *be* saved . . . ." The greatest difficulty spiritually is to concentrate on God, and His blessings are what make it so difficult. Troubles almost always make us look to God, but His blessings tend to divert our attention elsewhere. The basic lesson of the Sermon on the Mount is to narrow all your interests until your mind, heart, and body are focused on Jesus Christ. "Look to Me . . . ."

Many of us have a mental picture of what a Christian should be, and looking at this image in other Christians' lives becomes a hindrance to our focusing on God. This is not salvation—it is not simple enough. He says, in effect, "Look to Me and you are saved," not "You will be saved someday." We will find what we are looking for if we will concentrate on Him. We get distracted from God and irritable with Him while He continues to say to us, "Look to Me, and be saved . . . ." Our difficulties, our trials, and our worries about tomorrow all vanish when we look to God.

Wake yourself up and look to God. Build your hope on Him. No matter how many things seem to be pressing in on you, be determined to push them aside and look to Him. "Look to Me . . . ." Salvation is yours the moment you look.

Lord, unto You do I look up. How I know that "in me dwelleth no good thing"; and how marvelous is Your grace that I now find in my heart no motive save for Your glory.

Transformed by Beholding

"We all, with unveiled face, beholding as in a mirror the glory of the Lord, are being transformed into the same image . . . ."

—2 CORINTHIANS 3:18

The greatest characteristic a Christian can exhibit is this completely unveiled openness before God, which allows that person's life to become a mirror for others. When the Spirit fills us, we are transformed, and by beholding God we become mirrors. You can always tell when someone has been beholding the glory of the Lord, because your inner spirit senses that he mirrors the Lord's own character. Beware of anything that would spot or tarnish that mirror in you. It is almost always something good that will stain it—something good, but not what is best.

The most important rule for us is to concentrate on keeping our lives open to God. Let everything else including work, clothes, and food be set aside. The busyness of things obscures our concentration on God. We must maintain a position of beholding Him, keeping our lives completely spiritual through and through. Let other things come and go as they will; let other people criticize us as they will; but never allow anything to obscure the life that "is hidden with Christ in God" (Colossians 3:3). Never let a hurried lifestyle disturb the relationship of abiding in Him. This is an easy thing to allow, but we must guard against it. The most difficult lesson of the Christian life is learning how to continue "beholding as in a mirror the glory of the Lord . . . ."

O Lord, I look to you so utterly that I am worse than useless without You. Be made wisdom and discernment and understanding unto me today.

✑ DAY 10 ✑

God's Overpowering Purpose

"I have appeared to you for this purpose . . . ."   —ACTS 26:16

The vision Paul had on the road to Damascus was not a passing emotional experience, but a vision that had very clear and emphatic directions for him. And Paul stated, "I was not disobedient to the heavenly vision" (Acts 26:19). Our Lord said to Paul, in effect, "Your whole life is to be overpowered or subdued by Me; you are to have no end, no aim, and no purpose but Mine." And the Lord also says to us, "You did not choose Me, but *I chose you* and appointed you that you should go . . ." (John 15:16).

When we are born again, if we are spiritual at all, we have visions of what Jesus wants us to be. It is important that I learn not to be "disobedient to the heavenly vision"—not to doubt that it can be attained. It is not enough to give mental assent to the fact that God has redeemed the world, nor even to know that the Holy Spirit can make all that Jesus did a reality in my life. I must have the foundation of a personal relationship with Him. Paul was not given a message or a doctrine to proclaim. He was brought into a vivid, personal, overpowering relationship with Jesus Christ. Acts 26:16 is tremendously compelling ". . . to make you a minister and a witness . . . ." There would be nothing there without a personal relationship. Paul was devoted to a Person, not to a cause. He was absolutely Jesus Christ's. He saw nothing else and he lived for nothing else. "For I determined not to know anything among you except Jesus Christ and Him crucified" (1 Corinthians 2:2).

O Lord, enchain me to Yourself with great bonds of adoring love; encircle me around with Your Providence for Your purposes; enlarge me until I am more and more capable of being of use to You.

⸙ DAY 11 ⸙

Leave Room for God

"When it pleased God . . . ."   —GALATIANS 1:15

A s servants of God, we must learn to make room for Him—to give God "elbow room." We plan and figure and predict that this or that will happen, but we forget to make room for God to come in as He chooses. Would we be surprised if God came into our meeting or into our preaching in a way we had never expected Him to come? Do not look for God to come in a particular way, but *do look for Him.* The way to make room for Him is to expect Him to come, but not in a certain way. No matter how well we may know God, the great lesson to learn is that He may break in at any minute. We tend to overlook this element of surprise, yet God never works in any other way. Suddenly, God meets our life—"when it pleased God."

Keep your life so constantly in touch with God that His surprising power can break through at any point. Live in a constant state of expectancy, and leave room for God to come in as He decides.

Lord, breathe on me until my frame is knit to Your thought. Lift me until I see Your face and trust Your Almightiness without fear or insidious unbelief.

‏⌁ DAY 12 ⌁

Look Again and Consecrate

"If God so clothes the grass of the field . . . will He not much more clothe you . . . ?" —MATTHEW 6:30

A simple statement of Jesus is always a puzzle to us because we will not be simple. How can we maintain the simplicity of Jesus so that we may understand Him? By receiving His Spirit, recognizing and relying on Him, and obeying Him as He brings us the truth of His Word, life will become amazingly simple. Jesus asks us to consider that "if God so clothes the grass of the field . . ." how "much more" will He clothe you, if you keep your relationship right with Him? Every time we lose ground in our fellowship with God, it is because we have disrespectfully thought that we knew better than Jesus Christ. We have allowed "the cares of this world" to enter in (Matthew 13:22), while forgetting the "much more" of our heavenly Father.

"Look at the birds of the air . . ." (6:26). Their function is to obey the instincts God placed within them, and God watches over them. Jesus said that if you have the right relationship with Him and will obey His Spirit within you, then God will care for your "feathers" too.

"Consider the lilies of the field . . ." (6:28). They grow where they are planted. Many of us refuse to grow where God plants us. Therefore, we don't take root anywhere. Jesus said if we would obey the life of God within us, He would look after all other things. Did Jesus Christ lie to us? Are we experiencing the "much more" He promised? If we are not, it is because we are not obeying the life God has given us and have cluttered our minds with confusing thoughts and worries. How much time have we wasted asking God senseless questions while we should be absolutely free to concentrate on our service to Him? Consecration is the act of continually separating myself from everything except that which God has appointed me to do. It is not a one-time experience but an ongoing process. Am I continually separating myself and looking to God every day of my life?

O Lord, I praise You for the revelation of Your supreme Fatherhood that dawns on me through the grace of the Lord Jesus. Oh, that I may be the child of my Father in heaven!

☞ DAY 13 ☜

Look Again and Think

"Do not worry about your life . . . ."   —MATTHEW 6:25

A warning which needs to be repeated is that "the cares of this world and the deceitfulness of riches," and the lust for other things, will choke out the life of God in us (Matthew 13:22). We are never free from the recurring waves of this invasion. If the frontline of attack is not about clothes and food, it may be about money or the lack of money; or friends or lack of friends; or the line may be drawn over difficult circumstances. It is one steady invasion, and these things will come in like a flood, unless we allow the Spirit of God to raise up the banner against it.

"I say to you, do not worry about your life . . . ." Our Lord says to be careful only about one thing—our relationship to Him. But our common sense shouts loudly and says, "That is absurd, I *must* consider how I am going to live, and I *must* consider what I am going to eat and drink." Jesus says you must not. Beware of allowing yourself to think that He says this while not understanding your circumstances. Jesus Christ knows our circumstances better than we do, and He says we must not think about these things to the point where they become the primary concern of our life. Whenever there are competing concerns in your life, be sure you always put your relationship to God first.

"Sufficient for the day is its own trouble" (6:34). How much trouble has begun to threaten you today? What kind of mean little demons have been looking into your life and saying, "What are your plans for next month—or next summer?" Jesus tells us not to worry about any of these things. Look again and think. Keep your mind on the "much more" of your heavenly Father (6:30).

Detach me, O Lord, from the things of sense and time, and usher me into the presence of the King. Keep the precincts of my mind and heart entirely Yours.

⮐ DAY 14 ⮑

The Compelling Majesty of His Power

"The love of Christ compels us . . . ."   —2 CORINTHIANS 5:14

Paul said that he was overpowered, subdued, and held as in a vise by "the love of Christ." Very few of us really know what it means to be held in the grip of the love of God. We tend so often to be controlled simply by our own experience. The one thing that gripped and held Paul, to the exclusion of everything else, was the love of God. "The love of Christ compels us . . . ." When you hear that coming from the life of a man or woman it is unmistakable. You will know that the Spirit of God is completely unhindered in that person's life.

When we are born again by the Spirit of God, our testimony is based solely on what God has done for us, and rightly so. But that will change and be removed forever once you "receive power when the Holy Spirit has come upon you . . ." (Acts 1:8). Only then will you begin to realize what Jesus meant when He went on to say, ". . . you shall be *witnesses to Me* . . . ." Not witnesses to what Jesus can do—that is basic and understood—but "witnesses to Me . . . ." We will accept everything that happens as if it were happening to Him, whether we receive praise or blame, persecution or reward. No one is able to take this stand for Jesus Christ who is not totally compelled by the majesty of His power. It is the only thing that matters, and yet it is strange that it's the last thing we as Christian workers realize. Paul said that he was gripped by the love of God and that is why he acted as he did. People could perceive him as mad or sane—he did not care. There was only one thing he lived for—to persuade people of the coming judgment of God and to tell them of "the love of Christ." This total surrender to "the love of Christ" is the only thing that will bear fruit in your life. And it will always leave the mark of God's holiness and His power, never drawing attention to your personal holiness.

Draw me, O Lord, into vital communion with Yourself. Press through till I am thrilled with Your presence. Cause me to be Yours in the expression of Your grace as well as in the experience of it.

DAY 15

Our Misgivings About Jesus

"The woman said to Him, 'Sir, You have nothing to draw [water] with, and the well is deep.'"
—JOHN 4:11

Have you ever said to yourself, "I am impressed with the wonderful truths of God's Word, but He can't really expect me to live up to that and work all those details into my life!" When it comes to confronting Jesus Christ on the basis of His qualities and abilities, our attitudes reflect religious superiority. We think His ideals are lofty and they impress us, but we believe He is not in touch with reality—that what He says cannot actually be done. Each of us thinks this about Jesus in one area of our life or another. These doubts or misgivings about Jesus begin as we consider questions that divert our focus away from God. While we talk of our dealings with Him, others ask us, "Where are you going to get enough money to live? How will you live and who will take care of you?" Or our misgivings begin within ourselves when we tell Jesus that our circumstances are just a little too difficult for Him. We say, "It's easy to say, 'Trust in the Lord,' but a person has to live; and besides, Jesus has nothing with which to draw water—no means to be able to give us these things." And beware of exhibiting religious deceit by saying, "Oh, I have no misgivings about Jesus, only misgivings about myself." If we are honest, we will admit that we never have misgivings or doubts about ourselves, because we know exactly what we are capable or incapable of doing. But we do have misgivings about Jesus. And our pride is hurt even at the thought that He can do what we can't.

My misgivings arise from the fact that I search within to find how He will do what He says. My doubts spring from the depths of my own inferiority. If I detect these misgivings in myself, I should bring them into the light and confess them openly—"Lord, I have had misgivings about You. I have not believed in Your abilities, but only my own. And I have not believed in Your almighty power apart from my finite understanding of it."

O Lord, with what abundant relief I turn to You! I need You in unfathomable ways, and with what amazed relief and joy I find all I need in You.

The Impoverished Ministry of Jesus

"Where then do You get that living water?" —JOHN 4:11

The well is deep"—and even a great deal deeper than the Samaritan woman knew (4:11)! Think of the depths of human nature and human life; think of the depth of the "wells" in you. Have you been limiting, or impoverishing, the ministry of Jesus to the point that He is unable to work in your life? Suppose that you have a deep "well" of hurt and trouble inside your heart, and Jesus comes and says to you, "Let not your heart be troubled . . ." (John 14:1). Would your response be to shrug your shoulders and say, "But, Lord, the well is too deep, and even You can't draw up quietness and comfort out of it." Actually, that is correct. Jesus doesn't bring anything up from the wells of human nature—He brings them down from above. We limit the Holy One of Israel by remembering only what we have allowed Him to do for us in the past, and also by saying, "Of course, I cannot expect God to do this particular thing." The thing that approaches the very limits of His power is the very thing we as disciples of Jesus ought to believe He will do. We impoverish and weaken His ministry in us the moment we forget He is almighty. The impoverishment is in us, not in Him. We will come to Jesus for Him to be our comforter or our sympathizer, but we refrain from approaching Him as our Almighty God.

The reason some of us are such poor examples of Christianity is that we have failed to recognize that Christ is almighty. We have Christian attributes and experiences, but there is no abandonment or surrender to Jesus Christ. When we get into difficult circumstances, we impoverish His ministry by saying, "Of course, He can't do anything about this." We struggle to reach the bottom of our own well, trying to get water for ourselves. Beware of sitting back, and saying, "It can't be done." You will know it can be done if you will look to Jesus. The well of your incompleteness runs deep, but make the effort to look away from yourself and to look toward Him.

O Lord, what a wonder of perfect confidence it would create could I but hear some clear disposing word of Yours! Lord, speak it today.

"Do You Now Believe?"

" 'By this we believe . . . .' Jesus answered them, 'Do you now believe?' "
—JOHN 16:30–31

Now we believe. But Jesus asks, "Do you . . . ? Indeed the hour is coming . . . that you . . . will leave Me alone" (16:31–32). Many Christian workers have left Jesus Christ alone and yet tried to serve Him out of a sense of duty, or because they sense a need as a result of their own discernment. The reason for this is actually the absence of the resurrection life of Jesus. Our soul has gotten out of intimate contact with God by leaning on our own religious understanding (see Proverbs 3:5–6). This is not deliberate sin and there is no punishment attached to it. But once a person realizes how he has hindered his understanding of Jesus Christ, and caused uncertainties, sorrows, and difficulties for himself, it is with shame and remorse that he has to return.

We need to rely on the resurrection life of Jesus on a much deeper level than we do now. We should get in the habit of continually seeking His counsel on everything, instead of making our own commonsense decisions and then asking Him to bless them. He cannot bless them; it is not in His realm to do so, and those decisions are severed from reality. If we do something simply out of a sense of duty, we are trying to live up to a standard that competes with Jesus Christ. We become a prideful, arrogant person, thinking we know what to do in every situation. We have put our sense of duty on the throne of our life, instead of enthroning the resurrection life of Jesus. We are not told to "walk in the light" of our conscience or in the light of a sense of duty, but to "walk in the light *as He is in the light . . .*" (1 John 1:7). When we do something out of a sense of duty, it is easy to explain the reasons for our actions to others. But when we do something out of obedience to the Lord, there can be no other explanation—just obedience. That is why a saint can be so easily ridiculed and misunderstood.

O Lord, when I awake, I am still with You. Quicken my mortal body with Your mighty resurrection life; rouse me this hour with a gracious influx of power.

⟡ DAY 18 ⟡

What Do You Want the Lord
to Do for You?

*" 'What do you want Me to do for you?' He said, 'Lord, that I may
receive my sight.'"* —LUKE 18:41

Is there something in your life that not only disturbs you, but makes you
a disturbance to others? If so, it is always something you cannot han-
dle yourself. "Then those who went before warned him that he should be
quiet; but he cried out all the more . . ." (18:39). Be persistent with your
disturbance until you get face to face with the Lord Himself. Don't deify
common sense. To sit calmly by, instead of creating a disturbance, serves
only to deify our common sense. When Jesus asks what we want Him to
do for us about the incredible problem that is confronting us, remember
that He doesn't work in commonsense ways, but only in supernatural ways.

Look at how we limit the Lord by only remembering what we have
allowed Him to do for us in the past. We say, "I always failed there, and
I always will." Consequently, we don't ask for what we want. Instead, we
think, "It is ridiculous to ask God to do this." If it is an impossibility, it is
the very thing for which we have to ask. If it is not an impossible thing, it
is not a real disturbance. And God will do what is absolutely impossible.

This man received his sight. But the most impossible thing for you is
to be so closely identified with the Lord that there is literally nothing of
your old life remaining. God will do it if you will ask Him. But you have
to come to the point of believing Him to be almighty. We find faith by not
only believing what Jesus says, but, even more, by trusting Jesus Himself. If
we only look at what He says, we will never believe. Once we see Jesus, the
impossible things He does in our lives become as natural as breathing. The
agony we suffer is only the result of the deliberate shallowness of our own
heart. We *won't* believe; we *won't* let go by severing the line that secures the
boat to the shore—we prefer to worry.

---

*I praise You that all I am is Yours. Oh, that I could delight You as the lily does,
or the tree, or even the sparrows, just living the life You have granted!*

❧ DAY 19 ❧

The Piercing Question

"Do you love Me?"   —JOHN 21:17

Peter's response to this piercing question is considerably different from the bold defiance he exhibited only a few days before when he declared, "Even if I have to die with You, I will not deny You!" (Matthew 26:35; also see verses 33–34). Our natural individuality, or our natural self, boldly speaks out and declares its feelings. But the true love within our inner spiritual self can be discovered only by experiencing the hurt of this question of Jesus Christ. Peter loved Jesus in the way any natural man loves a good person. Yet that is nothing but emotional love. It may reach deeply into our natural self, but it never penetrates to the spirit of a person. True love never simply declares itself. Jesus said, "Whoever *confesses* Me before men [that is, confesses his love by everything he does, not merely by his words], him the Son of Man also will confess before the angels of God" (Luke 12:8).

Unless we are experiencing the hurt of facing every deception about ourselves, we have hindered the work of the Word of God in our lives. The Word of God inflicts hurt on us more than sin ever could, because sin dulls our senses. But this question of the Lord intensifies our sensitivities to the point that this hurt produced by Jesus is the most exquisite pain conceivable. It hurts not only on the natural level, but also on the deeper spiritual level. "For the Word of God is living and powerful . . . , piercing even to the division of soul and spirit . . ."—to the point that no deception can remain (Hebrews 4:12). When the Lord asks us this question, it is impossible to think and respond properly, because when the Lord speaks directly to us, the pain is too intense. It causes such a tremendous hurt that any part of our life which may be out of line with His will can feel the pain. There is never any mistaking the pain of the Lord's Word by His children, but the moment that pain is felt is the very moment at which God reveals His truth to us.

O Lord, this morning disperse every mist. Shine forth clear and strong and invigoratingly.

❧ DAY 20 ❧

Have You Felt the Pain Inflicted by the Lord?

"He said to him the third time, '. . . do you love Me?'" —JOHN 21:17

Have you ever felt the pain, inflicted by the Lord, at the very center of your being, deep down in the most sensitive area of your life? The devil never inflicts pain there, and neither can sin nor human emotions.

Nothing can cut through to that part of our being but the Word of God. "Peter was grieved because He said to him the third time, 'Do you love Me?'" Yet he was awakened to the fact that at the center of his personal life he was devoted to Jesus. And then he began to see what Jesus' patient questioning meant. There was not the slightest bit of doubt left in Peter's mind; he could never be deceived again. And there was no need for an impassioned response; no need for immediate action or an emotional display. It was a revelation to him to realize how much he did love the Lord, and with amazement he simply said, "Lord, You know all things . . . ." Peter began to see how very much he did love Jesus, and there was no need to say, "Look at this or that as proof of my love." Peter was beginning to discover within himself just how much he really did love the Lord. He discovered that his eyes were so fixed on Jesus Christ that he saw no one else in heaven above or on the earth below. But he did not know it until the probing, hurting questions of the Lord were asked. The Lord's questions always reveal the true me to myself.

Oh, the wonder of the patient directness and skill of Jesus Christ with Peter! Our Lord never asks questions until the perfect time. Rarely, but probably once in each of our lives, He will back us into a corner where He will hurt us with His piercing questions. Then we will realize that we do love Him far more deeply than our words can ever say.

O Lord, You have enlarged me when I was in distress. Oh, that the thoughts of my heart were more and more a well-spring of gracious treasure without ceasing!

⤖ DAY 21 ⤖

His Commission to Us

"Feed My sheep."   —JOHN 21:17

This is love in the making. The love of God is not created—it is His nature. When we receive the life of Christ through the Holy Spirit, He unites us with God so that His love is demonstrated in us. The goal of the indwelling Holy Spirit is not just to unite us with God, but to do it in such a way that we will be one with the Father in exactly the same way Jesus was. And what kind of oneness did Jesus Christ have with the Father? He had such a oneness with the Father that He was obedient when His Father sent Him down here to be poured out for us. And He says to us, "As the Father has sent Me, I also send you" (John 20:21).

Peter now realizes that he does love Him, due to the revelation that came with the Lord's piercing question. The Lord's next point is—"Pour yourself out. Don't testify about how much you love Me and don't talk about the wonderful revelation you have had, just 'Feed My sheep.'" Jesus has some extraordinarily peculiar sheep: some that are unkempt and dirty, some that are awkward or pushy, and some that have gone astray! But it is impossible to exhaust God's love, and it is impossible to exhaust my love if it flows from the Spirit of God within me. The love of God pays no attention to my prejudices caused by my natural individuality. If I love my Lord, I have no business being guided by natural emotions—I have to feed His sheep. We will not be delivered or released from His commission to us. Beware of counterfeiting the love of God by following your own natural human emotions, sympathies, or understandings. That will only serve to revile and abuse the true love of God.

I would, O Lord, have all my thoughts and emotions and words redolent with love, perfect love to You, and through that to others.

∽ DAY 22 ∾

Is This True of Me?

"None of these things move me; nor do I count my life dear to myself
. . . ."
                                                    —ACTS 20:24

It is easier to serve or work for God without a vision and without a call, because then you are not bothered by what He requires. Common sense, covered with a layer of Christian emotion, becomes your guide. You may be more prosperous and successful from the world's perspective, and will have more leisure time, if you never acknowledge the call of God. But once you receive a commission from Jesus Christ, the memory of what God asks of you will always be there to prod you on to do His will. You will no longer be able to work for Him on the basis of common sense.

What do I count in my life as "dear to myself"? If I have not been seized by Jesus Christ and have not surrendered myself to Him, I will consider the time I decide to give God and my own ideas of service as dear. I will also consider my own life as "dear to myself." But Paul said he considered his life dear so that he might fulfill the ministry he had received, and he refused to use his energy on anything else. This verse shows an almost noble annoyance by Paul at being asked to consider himself. He was absolutely indifferent to any consideration other than that of fulfilling the ministry he had received. Our ordinary and reasonable service to God may actually compete against our total surrender to Him. Our reasonable work is based on the following argument which we say to ourselves, "Remember how useful you are here, and think how much value you would be in that particular type of work." That attitude chooses our own judgment, instead of Jesus Christ, to be our guide as to where we should go and where we could be used the most. Never consider whether or not you are of use—but always consider that "you are not your own" (1 Corinthians 6:19). You are His.

O Lord, by Your grace open my vision to You and Your infinite horizons, and take me into Your counsels regarding Your work in this place.

≈ DAY 23 ≈

Is He Really My Lord?

". . . so that I may finish my race with joy, and the ministry which I received from the Lord Jesus . . . ." —ACTS 20:24

Joy comes from seeing the complete fulfillment of the specific purpose for which I was created and born again, not from successfully doing something of my own choosing. The joy our Lord experienced came from doing what the Father sent Him to do. And He says to us, "As the Father has sent Me, I also send you" (John 20:21). Have you received a ministry from the Lord? If so, you must be faithful to it—to consider your life valuable only for the purpose of fulfilling that ministry. Knowing that you have done what Jesus sent you to do, think how satisfying it will be to hear Him say to you, "Well done, good and faithful servant" (Matthew 25:21). We each have to find a niche in life, and spiritually we find it when we receive a ministry from the Lord. To do this we must have close fellowship with Jesus and must know Him as more than our personal Savior. And we must be willing to experience the full impact of Acts 9:16—"I will show him how many things he must suffer *for My name's sake.*"

"Do you love Me?" Then, "Feed My sheep" (John 21:17). He is not offering us a choice of how we can serve Him; He is asking for absolute loyalty to His commission, a faithfulness to what we discern when we are in the closest possible fellowship with God. If you have received a ministry from the Lord Jesus, you will know that the need is not the same as the call—the need is the opportunity to exercise the call. The call is to be faithful to the ministry you received when you were in true fellowship with Him. This does not imply that there is a whole series of differing ministries marked out for you. It does mean that you must be sensitive to what God has called you to do, and this may sometimes require ignoring demands for service in other areas.

O Lord, I beseech You for sustaining strength and simple joy. Keep me humble-minded in motive and design that nothing of the superior person may be mine.

✒ DAY 24 ✒

Taking the Next Step

". . . in much patience, in tribulations, in needs, in distresses."
—2 CORINTHIANS 6:4

When you have no vision from God, no enthusiasm left in your life, and no one watching and encouraging you, it requires the grace of Almighty God to take the next step in your devotion to Him, in the reading and studying of His Word, in your family life, or in your duty to Him. It takes much more of the grace of God, and a much greater awareness of drawing upon Him, to take that next step, than it does to preach the gospel.

Every Christian must experience the essence of the incarnation by bringing the next step down into flesh-and-blood reality and by working it out with his hands. We lose interest and give up when we have no vision, no encouragement, and no improvement, but only experience our everyday life with its trivial tasks. The thing that really testifies for God and for the people of God in the long run is steady perseverance, even when the work cannot be seen by others. And the only way to live an undefeated life is to live looking to God. Ask God to keep the eyes of your spirit open to the risen Christ, and it will be impossible for drudgery to discourage you. Never allow yourself to think that some tasks are beneath your dignity or too insignificant for you to do, and remind yourself of the example of Christ in John 13:1–17.

O Lord, save us from the murmuring spirit, which is harmful, hurting the bloom of spiritual communion.

☙ DAY 25 ❧
The Source of Abundant Joy

"In all these things we are more than conquerors through Him who loved us."
—ROMANS 8:37

Paul was speaking here of the things that might seem likely to separate a saint from the love of God. But the remarkable thing is that nothing *can* come between the love of God and a saint. The things Paul mentioned in this passage can and do disrupt the close fellowship of our soul with God and separate our natural life from Him. But none of them is able to come between the love of God and the soul of a saint on the spiritual level. The underlying foundation of the Christian faith is the undeserved, limitless miracle of the love of God that was exhibited on the Cross of Calvary; a love that is not earned and can never be. Paul said this is the reason that "in all these things we are more than conquerors." We are super-victors with a joy that comes from experiencing the very things which look as if they are going to overwhelm us.

Huge waves that would frighten an ordinary swimmer produce a tremendous thrill for the surfer who has ridden them. Let's apply that to our own circumstances. The things we try to avoid and fight against—tribulation, suffering, and persecution—are the very things that produce abundant joy in us. "We are more than conquerors through Him" "*in* all these things"; not in spite of them, but in the midst of them. A saint doesn't know the joy of the Lord in spite of tribulation, but *because* of it. Paul said, "I am exceedingly joyful in all our tribulation" (2 Corinthians 7:4).

The undiminished radiance, which is the result of abundant joy, is not built on anything passing, but on the love of God that nothing can change. And the experiences of life, whether they are everyday events or terrifying ones, are powerless to "separate us from the love of God which is in Christ Jesus our Lord" (Romans 8:39).

Lord, I praise You for the joy of my life here—for the love of wife and child, for the students, for the favors of the Holy Spirit. What a wonder of joy and radiant blessing this place has been!

The Surrendered Life

"I have been crucified with Christ . . . ."   —GALATIANS 2:20

To become one with Jesus Christ, a person must be willing not only to give up sin, but also to surrender his whole way of looking at things. Being born again by the Spirit of God means that we must first be willing to let go before we can grasp something else. The first thing we must surrender is all of our pretense or deceit. What our Lord wants us to present to Him is not our goodness, honesty, or our efforts to do better, but real solid sin. Actually, that is all He can take from us. And what He gives us in exchange for our sin is real solid righteousness. But we must surrender all pretense that we are anything, and give up all our claims of even being worthy of God's consideration.

Once we have done that, the Spirit of God will show us what we need to surrender next. Along each step of this process, we will have to give up our claims to our rights to ourselves. Are we willing to surrender our grasp on all that we possess, our desires, and everything else in our lives? Are we ready to be identified with the death of Jesus Christ?

We will suffer a sharp painful disillusionment before we fully surrender. When people really see themselves as the Lord sees them, it is not the terribly offensive sins of the flesh that shock them, but the awful nature of the pride of their own hearts opposing Jesus Christ. When they see themselves in the light of the Lord, the shame, horror, and desperate conviction hit home for them.

If you are faced with the question of whether or not to surrender, make a determination to go on through the crisis, surrendering all that you have and all that you are to Him. And God will then equip you to do all that He requires of you.

―――――――――

Breath on me, Breath of God, until my mind and spirit are in suitable adjustment to You. Shed abroad liberty and purity and power among and in us all.

⌐ DAY 27 ⌐

Turning Back or Walking with Jesus

"Do you also want to go away?"   —JOHN 6:67

What a penetrating question! Our Lord's words often hit home for us when He speaks in the simplest way. In spite of the fact that we know who Jesus is, He asks, "Do you also want to go away?" We must continually maintain an adventurous attitude toward Him, despite any potential personal risk.

"From that time many of His disciples went back and walked with Him no more" (6:66). They turned back from walking with Jesus; not into sin, but away from Him. Many people today are pouring their lives out and working for Jesus Christ, but are not really walking with Him. One thing God constantly requires of us is a oneness with Jesus Christ. After being set apart through sanctification, we should discipline our lives spiritually to maintain this intimate oneness. When God gives you a clear determination of His will for you, all your striving to maintain that relationship by some particular method is completely unnecessary. All that is required is to live a natural life of absolute dependence on Jesus Christ. Never try to live your life with God in any other way than His way. And His way means absolute devotion to Him. Showing no concern for the uncertainties that lie ahead is the secret of walking with Jesus.

Peter saw in Jesus only someone who could minister salvation to him and to the world. But our Lord wants us to be fellow laborers with Him.

In verse 70 Jesus lovingly reminded Peter that he was chosen to go with Him. And each of us must answer this question for ourselves and no one else: "Do you also want to go away?"

Lord, how little nourishment I have been giving to the indwelling Christ in me; O Lord, forgive me. Fill me with the ample sense of Your forgiveness that I may not only joy in Your salvation, but be filled with Your Spirit for the work You have given me to do.

☞ DAY 28 ☜

Being an Example of His Message

"Preach the word!"   —2 TIMOTHY 4:2

We are not saved only to be instruments for God, but to be His sons and daughters. He does not turn us into spiritual agents but into spiritual messengers, and the message must be a part of us. The Son of God was His own message—"The words that I speak to you are spirit, and they are life" (John 6:63). As His disciples, our lives must be a holy example of the reality of our message. Even the natural heart of the unsaved will serve if called upon to do so, but it takes a heart broken by conviction of sin, baptized by the Holy Spirit, and crushed into submission to God's purpose to make a person's life a holy example of God's message.

There is a difference between giving a testimony and preaching. A preacher is someone who has received the call of God and is determined to use all his energy to proclaim God's truth. God takes us beyond our own aspirations and ideas for our lives, and molds and shapes us for His purpose, just as He worked in the disciples' lives after Pentecost. The purpose of Pentecost was not to teach the disciples something, but to make them the incarnation of what they preached so that they would literally become God's message in the flesh. ". . . you shall be witnesses to Me . . ." (Acts 1:8).

Allow God to have complete liberty in your life when you speak. Before God's message can liberate other people, His liberation must first be real in you. Gather your material carefully, and then allow God to "set your words on fire" for His glory.

Lord God Omniscient, give me wisdom this day to worship and work aright and be well-pleasing to You. Lord, interpret Yourself to me more and more in Your fullness and beauty.

Obedience to the "Heavenly Vision"

"I was not disobedient to the heavenly vision."　　　　—ACTS 26:19

If we lose "the heavenly vision" God has given us, we alone are responsible—not God. We lose the vision because of our own lack of spiritual growth. If we do not apply our beliefs about God to the issues of everyday life, the vision God has given us will never be fulfilled. The only way to be obedient to "the heavenly vision" is to give our utmost for His highest—our best for His glory. This can be accomplished only when we make a determination to continually remember God's vision. But the acid test is obedience to the vision in the details of our everyday life—sixty seconds out of every minute, and sixty minutes out of every hour, not just during times of personal prayer or public meetings.

"Though it tarries, wait for it . . ." (Habakkuk 2:3). We cannot bring the vision to fulfillment through our own efforts, but must live under its inspiration until it fulfills itself. We try to be so practical that we forget the vision. At the very beginning we saw the vision but did not wait for it. We rushed off to do our practical work, and once the vision was fulfilled we could no longer even see it. Waiting for a vision that "tarries" is the true test of our faithfulness to God. It is at the risk of our own soul's welfare that we get caught up in practical busy-work, only to miss the fulfillment of the vision.

Watch for the storms of God. The only way God plants His saints is through the whirlwind of His storms. Will you be proven to be an empty pod with no seed inside? That will depend on whether or not you are actually living in the light of the vision you have seen. Let God send you out through His storm, and don't go until He does. If you select your own spot to be planted, you will prove yourself to be an unproductive, empty pod. However, if you allow God to plant you, you will "bear much fruit" (John 15:8).

It is essential that we live and "walk in the light" of God's vision for us (1 John 1:7).

In all matters, O Lord, I would acknowledge You. Keep me in tune with You so that others may catch the joyousness and gladness of God.

Total Surrender

"Peter began to say to Him, 'See, we have left all and followed You.'"
—MARK 10:28

Our Lord replies to this statement of Peter by saying that this surrender is "for My sake and the gospel's" (10:29). It was not for the purpose of what the disciples themselves would get out of it. Beware of surrender that is motivated by personal benefits that may result. For example, "I'm going to give myself to God because I want to be delivered from sin, because I want to be made holy." Being delivered from sin and being made holy are the result of being right with God, but surrender resulting from this kind of thinking is certainly not the true nature of Christianity. Our motive for surrender should not be *for* any personal gain at all. We have become so self-centered that we go to God only for something from Him, and not for God Himself. It is like saying, "No, Lord, I don't want you; I want myself. But I do want You to clean me and fill me with Your Holy Spirit. I want to be on display in Your showcase so I can say, 'This is what God has done for me.'" Gaining heaven, being delivered from sin, and being made useful to God are things that should never even be a consideration in real surrender. Genuine total surrender is a personal sovereign preference for Jesus Christ Himself.

Where does Jesus Christ figure in when we have a concern about our natural relationships? Most of us will desert Him with this excuse—"Yes, Lord, I heard you call me, but my family needs me and I have my own interests. I just can't go any further" (see Luke 9:57–62). "Then," Jesus says, "you 'cannot be My disciple'" (see Luke 14:26–33).

True surrender will always go beyond natural devotion. If we will only give up, God will surrender Himself to embrace all those around us and will meet their needs, which were created by our surrender. Beware of stopping anywhere short of total surrender to God. Most of us have only a vision of what this really means, but have never truly experienced it.

O Lord, cause my intellect to glow with Your Holy Spirit's teaching.

God's Total Surrender to Us

"For God so loved the world that He gave . . . ." —JOHN 3:16

Salvation does not mean merely deliverance from sin or the experience of personal holiness. The salvation which comes from God means being completely delivered from myself, and being placed into perfect union with Him. When I think of my salvation experience, I think of being delivered from sin and gaining personal holiness. But salvation is so much more! It means that the Spirit of God has brought me into intimate contact with the true Person of God Himself. And as I am caught up into total surrender to God, I become thrilled with something infinitely greater than myself.

To say that we are called to preach holiness or sanctification is to miss the main point. We are called to proclaim Jesus Christ (see 1 Corinthians 2:2). The fact that He saves from sin and makes us holy is actually part of the effect of His wonderful and total surrender to us.

If we are truly surrendered, we will never be aware of our own efforts to remain surrendered. Our entire life will be consumed with the One to whom we surrender. Beware of talking about surrender if you know nothing about it. In fact, you will never know anything about it until you understand that John 3:16 means that God completely and absolutely gave Himself to us. In our surrender, we must give ourselves to God in the same way He gave Himself for us—totally, unconditionally, and without reservation. The consequences and circumstances resulting from our surrender will never even enter our mind, because our life will be totally consumed with Him.

O Lord, I praise You for all the past—so wayward on my part, so gracious and longsuffering and forgiving and tender on Yours.

DAY 32

Yielding

". . . you are that one's slaves whom you obey . . . ."

—ROMANS 6:16

The first thing I must be willing to admit when I begin to examine what controls and dominates me is that I am the one responsible for having yielded myself to whatever it may be. If I am a slave to myself, I am to blame because somewhere in the past I yielded to myself. Likewise, if I obey God I do so because at some point in my life I yielded myself to Him. If a child gives in to selfishness, he will find it to be the most enslaving tyranny on earth. There is no power within the human soul itself that is capable of breaking the bondage of the nature created by yielding. For example, yield for one second to anything in the nature of lust, and although you may hate yourself for having yielded, you become enslaved to that thing. (Remember what lust is—"I must have it now," whether it is the lust of the flesh or the lust of the mind.) No release or escape from it will ever come from any human power, but only through the power of redemption. You must yield yourself in utter humiliation to the only One who can break the dominating power in your life, namely, the Lord Jesus Christ. ". . . He has anointed Me . . . to proclaim liberty to the captives . . ." (Luke 4:18 and Isaiah 61:1).

When you yield to something, you will soon realize the tremendous control it has over you. Even though you say, "Oh, I can give up that habit whenever I like," you will know you can't. You will find that the habit absolutely dominates you because you willingly yielded to it. It is easy to sing, "He will break every fetter," while at the same time living a life of obvious slavery to yourself. But yielding to Jesus will break every kind of slavery in any person's life.

O Lord, I do praise You that through Christ Jesus it is mercy and lovingkindness, graciousness and wonders, all along the way. I would I were more sensitive to You and Your doings, more Christlike in my gratitude.

42

⇌ DAY 33 ⇌

Abraham's Life of Faith

"He went out, not knowing where he was going."

—HEBREWS 11:8

In the Old Testament, a person's relationship with God was seen by the degree of separation in that person's life. This separation is exhibited in the life of Abraham by his separation from his country and his family. When we think of separation today, we do not mean to be literally separated from those family members who do not have a personal relationship with God, but to be separated mentally and morally from their viewpoints. This is what Jesus Christ was referring to in Luke 14:26.

Living a life of faith means never knowing where you are being led. But it does mean loving and knowing the One who is leading. It is literally a life of *faith*, not of understanding and reason—a life of knowing Him who calls us to go. Faith is rooted in the knowledge of a Person, and one of the biggest traps we fall into is the belief that if we have faith, God will surely lead us to success in the world.

The final stage in the life of faith is the attainment of character, and we encounter many changes in the process. We feel the presence of God around us when we pray, yet we are only momentarily changed. We tend to keep going back to our everyday ways and the glory vanishes. A life of faith is not a life of one glorious mountaintop experience after another, like soaring on eagles' wings, but is a life of day-in and day-out consistency; a life of walking without fainting (see Isaiah 40:31). It is not even a question of the holiness of sanctification, but of something which comes much farther down the road. It is a faith that has been tried and proved and has withstood the test. Abraham is not a type or an example of the holiness of sanctification, but a type of the life of faith—a faith, tested and true, built on the true God. *"Abraham believed God . . ."* (Romans 4:3).

O Lord, may this day be right glorious with Your presence and blessing. May Your presence cause me to walk without fainting.

❧ DAY 34 ❧

Friendship with God

"Shall I hide from Abraham what I am doing . . . ?" —GENESIS 18:17

The Delights of His Friendship. Genesis 18 brings out the delight of true friendship with God, as compared with simply feeling His presence occasionally in prayer. This friendship means being so intimately in touch with God that you never even need to ask Him to show you His will. It is evidence of a level of intimacy which confirms that you are nearing the final stage of your discipline in the life of faith. When you have a right-standing relationship with God, you have a life of freedom, liberty, and delight; you *are* God's will. And all of your commonsense decisions are actually His will for you, unless you sense a feeling of restraint brought on by a check in your spirit. You are free to make decisions in the light of a perfect and delightful friendship with God, knowing that if your decisions are wrong He will lovingly produce that sense of restraint. Once he does, you must stop immediately.

The Difficulties of His Friendship. Why did Abraham stop praying when he did? He stopped because he still was lacking the level of intimacy in his relationship with God, which would enable him boldly to continue on with the Lord in prayer until his desire was granted. Whenever we stop short of our true desire in prayer and say, "Well, I don't know, maybe this is not God's will," then we still have another level to go. It shows that we are not as intimately acquainted with God as Jesus was, and as Jesus would have us to be—". . . that they may be one just as We are one . . ." (John 17:22). Think of the last thing you prayed about—were you devoted to your desire or to God? Was your determination to get some gift of the Spirit for yourself or to get to God? "For your Father knows the things you have need of before you ask Him" (Matthew 6:8). The reason for asking is so you may get to know God better. "Delight yourself also in the Lord, and He shall give you the desires of your heart" (Psalm 37:4). We should keep praying to get a perfect understanding of God Himself.

O Lord, how wonderful are Your ways! When I recall the way You have led me and borne with me, I am lost in wonder, love, and praise.

↤ DAY 35 ↦

Take the Initiative

". . . add to your faith virtue . . . ."   —2 PETER 1:5

Add means that we have to do something. We are in danger of forget-ting that we cannot do what God does, and that God will not do what we can do. We cannot save nor sanctify ourselves—God does that. But God will not give us good habits or character, and He will not force us to walk correctly before Him. We have to do all that ourselves. We must "work *out*" our "own salvation" which God has worked *in* us (Philippians 2:12). *Add* means that we must get into the habit of doing things, and in the initial stages that is difficult. To take the initiative is to make a begin-ning—to instruct yourself in the way you must go.

Beware of the tendency to ask the way when you know it perfectly well. Take the initiative—stop hesitating—take the first step. Be determined to act immediately in faith on what God says to you when He speaks, and never reconsider or change your initial decisions. If you hesitate when God tells you to do something, you are being careless, spurning the grace in which you stand. Take the initiative yourself, make a decision of your will right now, and make it impossible to go back. Burn your bridges behind you, saying, "I *will* write that letter," or "I *will* pay that debt"; and then do it! Make it irrevocable.

We have to get into the habit of carefully listening to God about every-thing, forming the habit of finding out what He says and heeding it. If, when a crisis comes, we instinctively turn to God, we will know that the habit has been formed in us. We have to take the initiative where we *are*, not where we have not yet been.

O Lord, that more passionate, devout, and earnest love to You might show itself in my conscious life. Oh, for grace to show and to feel patience and gentleness to those around me!

⌁ DAY 36 ⌁

"Love One Another"

". . . add to your . . . brotherly kindness love." —2 PETER 1:5, 7

Love is an indefinite thing to most of us; we don't know what we mean when we talk about love. Love is the loftiest preference of one person for another, and spiritually Jesus demands that this sovereign preference be for Himself (see Luke 14:26). Initially, when "the love of God has been poured out in our hearts by the Holy Spirit" (Romans 5:5), it is easy to put Jesus first. But then we must practice the things mentioned in 2 Peter 1 to see them worked out in our lives.

The first thing God does is forcibly remove any insincerity, pride, and vanity from my life. And the Holy Spirit reveals to me that God loved me not because I was lovable, but because it was His nature to do so. Now He commands me to show the same love to others by saying, ". . . love one another as I have loved you" (John 15:12). He is saying, "I will bring a number of people around you whom you cannot respect, but you must exhibit My love to them, just as I have exhibited it to you." This kind of love is not a patronizing love for the unlovable—it is His love, and it will not be evidenced in us overnight. Some of us may have tried to force it, but we were soon tired and frustrated.

"The Lord . . . is longsuffering toward us, not willing that any should perish . . ." (2 Peter 3:9). I should look within and remember how wonderfully He has dealt with me. The knowledge that God has loved me beyond all limits will compel me to go into the world to love others in the same way. I may get irritated because I have to live with an unusually difficult person. But just think how disagreeable I have been with God! Am I prepared to be identified so closely with the Lord Jesus that His life and His sweetness will be continually poured out through Me? Neither natural love nor God's divine love will remain and grow in me unless it is nurtured. Love is spontaneous, but it has to be maintained through discipline.

O Lord, touch my life with Your energizing power and loving-kindness and beauty. Make it a time of the unveiling of Your face.

The Habit of Having No Habits

"If these things are yours and abound, you will be neither barren nor unfruitful." —2 PETER 1:8

When we first begin to form a habit, we are fully aware of it. There are times when we are aware of becoming virtuous and godly, but this awareness should only be a stage we quickly pass through as we grow spiritually. If we stop at this stage, we will develop a sense of spiritual pride. The right thing to do with godly habits is to immerse them in the life of the Lord until they become such a spontaneous expression of our lives that we are no longer aware of them. Our spiritual life continually causes us to focus our attention inwardly for the determined purpose of self-examination, because each of us has some qualities we have not yet added to our lives.

Your god may be your little Christian habit—the habit of prayer or Bible reading at certain times of your day. Watch how your Father will upset your schedule if you begin to worship your habit instead of what the habit symbolizes. We say, "I can't do that right now; this is my time alone with God." No, this is your time alone with your habit. There is a quality that is still lacking in you. Identify your shortcoming and then look for opportunities to work into your life that missing quality.

Love means that there are no visible habits—that your habits are so immersed in the Lord that you practice them without realizing it. If you are consciously aware of your own holiness, you place limitations on yourself from doing certain things—things God is not restricting you from at all. This means there is a missing quality that needs to be added to your life. The only supernatural life is the life the Lord Jesus lived, and He was at home with God anywhere. Is there someplace where you are not at home with God? Then allow God to work through whatever that particular circumstance may be until you increase in Him, adding His qualities. Your life will then become the simple life of a child.

O Lord, open Your truths to our understanding and keep us strong in You.

☙ DAY 38 ☙

The Habit of Keeping
a Clear Conscience

". . . strive to have a conscience without offense toward God and men."
—ACTS 24:16

God's commands to us are actually given to the life of His Son in us. Consequently, to our human nature in which God's Son has been formed (see Galatians 4:19), His commands are difficult. But they become divinely easy once we obey.

Conscience is that ability within me that attaches itself to the highest standard I know, and then continually reminds me of what that standard demands that I do. It is the eye of the soul which looks out either toward God or toward what we regard as the highest standard. This explains why conscience is different in different people. If I am in the habit of continually holding God's standard in front of me, my conscience will always direct me to God's perfect law and indicate what I should do. The question is, will I obey? I have to make an effort to keep my conscience so sensitive that I can live without any offense toward anyone. I should be living in such perfect harmony with God's Son that the spirit of my mind is being renewed through every circumstance of life, and that I may be able to quickly "prove what is that good and acceptable and perfect will of God" (Romans 12:2; also see Ephesians 4:23).

God always instructs us down to the last detail. Is my ear sensitive enough to hear even the softest whisper of the Spirit, so that I know what I should do? "Do not grieve the Holy Spirit of God . . ." (Ephesians 4:30). He does not speak with a voice like thunder—His voice is so gentle that it is easy for us to ignore. And the only thing that keeps our conscience sensitive to Him is the habit of being open to God on the inside. When you begin to debate, stop immediately. Don't ask, "Why can't I do this?" You are on the wrong track. There is no debating possible once your conscience speaks. Whatever it is—drop it, and see that you keep your inner vision clear.

Lord, touch me physically with Your well-being, and may I be filled with praise.

∼ DAY 39 ∼
The Habit of Enjoying Adversity

". . . that the life of Jesus also may be manifested in our body."
—2 CORINTHIANS 4:10

We have to develop godly habits to express what God's grace has done in us. It is not just a question of being saved from hell, but of being saved so that "the life of Jesus also may be manifested in our body." And it is adversity that makes us exhibit His life in our mortal flesh. Is my life exhibiting the essence of the sweetness of the Son of God, or just the basic irritation of "myself" that I would have apart from Him? The only thing that will enable me to enjoy adversity is the acute sense of eagerness of allowing the life of the Son of God to evidence itself in me. No matter how difficult something may be, I must say, "Lord, I am delighted to obey You in this." Instantly, the Son of God will move to the forefront of my life, and will manifest in my body that which glorifies Him.

You must not debate. The moment you obey the light of God, His Son shines through you in that very adversity; but if you debate with God, you grieve His Spirit (see Ephesians 4:30). You must keep yourself in the proper condition to allow the life of the Son of God to be manifested in you, and you cannot keep yourself fit if you give way to self-pity. Our circumstances are the means God uses to exhibit just how wonderfully perfect and extraordinarily pure His Son is. Discovering a new way of manifesting the Son of God should make our heart beat with renewed excitement. It is one thing to choose adversity, and quite another to enter into adversity through the orchestrating of our circumstances by God's sovereignty. And if God puts you into adversity, He is adequately sufficient to "supply all your need" (Philippians 4:19).

Keep your soul properly conditioned to manifest the life of the Son of God. Never live on your memories of past experiences, but let the Word of God always be living and active in you.

Your ways, O Lord, are like Yourself—perfect. My ways are like myself—imperfect. Bring me into conscious identity with You and with Your ways for this day.

⪧ DAY 40 ⪦

The Habit of Rising to the Occasion

". . . that you may know what is the hope of His calling . . . ."
—EPHESIANS 1:18

Remember that you have been saved so that the life of Jesus may be manifested in your body (see 2 Corinthians 4:10). Direct the total energy of your powers so that you may achieve everything your election as a child of God provides; rise every time to whatever occasion may come your way.

You did not do anything to achieve your salvation, but you must do something to exhibit it. You must "work *out* your own salvation" which God has worked *in* you already (Philippians 2:12). Are your speech, your thinking, and your emotions evidence that you are working it "out"? If you are still the same miserable, grouchy person, set on having your own way, then it is a lie to say that God has saved and sanctified you.

God is the Master Designer, and He allows adversities into your life to see if you can jump over them properly—"By my God I can leap over a wall" (Psalm 18:29). God will never shield you from the requirements of being His son or daughter. First Peter 4:12 says, "Beloved, do not think it strange concerning the fiery trial which is to try you, as though some strange thing happened to you . . . ." Rise to the occasion—do what the trial demands of you. It does not matter how much it hurts as long as it gives God the opportunity to manifest the life of Jesus in your body.

May God not find complaints in us anymore, but spiritual vitality—a readiness to face anything He brings our way. The only proper goal of life is that we manifest the Son of God; and when this occurs, all of our dictating of our demands to God disappears. Our Lord never dictated demands to His Father, and neither are we to make demands on God. We are here to submit to His will so that He may work through us what He wants. Once we realize this, He will make us broken bread and poured-out wine with which to feed and nourish others.

Lord, so much truth revealed, so many things to say, and so little do I feel I live up to what You show me. Lord, empower me for Your glory.

⌐ DAY 41 ⌐

The Habit of Recognizing God's Provision

". . . you may be partakers of the divine nature . . . ." —2 PETER 1:4

We are made "partakers of the divine nature," receiving and sharing God's own nature through His promises. Then we have to work that divine nature into our human nature by developing godly habits. The first habit to develop is the habit of recognizing God's provision for us. We say, however, "Oh, I can't afford it." One of the worst lies is wrapped up in that statement. We talk as if our heavenly Father has cut us off without a penny! We think it is a sign of true humility to say at the end of the day, "Well, I just barely got by today, but it was a severe struggle." And yet all of Almighty God is ours in the Lord Jesus! And He will reach to the last grain of sand and the remotest star to bless us if we will only obey Him. Does it really matter that our circumstances are difficult? Why shouldn't they be! If we give way to self-pity and indulge in the luxury of misery, we remove God's riches from our lives and hinder others from entering into His provision. No sin is worse than the sin of self-pity, because it removes God from the throne of our lives, replacing Him with our own self-interests. It causes us to open our mouths only to complain, and we simply become spiritual sponges—always absorbing, never giving, and never being satisfied. And there is nothing lovely or generous about our lives.

Before God becomes satisfied with us, He will take everything of our so-called wealth, until we learn that He is our Source; as the psalmist said, "All my springs are in You" (Psalm 87:7). If the majesty, grace, and power of God are not being exhibited in us, God holds us responsible. "God is able to make all grace abound toward you, that you . . . may have an abundance . . ." (2 Corinthians 9:8)—then learn to lavish the grace of God on others, generously giving of yourself. Be marked and identified with God's nature, and His blessing will flow through you all the time.

Lord, bring the sweetness and fullness of Your power to bear on me this day. Oh, for the big, the generous, the gracious life of God!

⌒ DAY 42 ⌒

His Ascension and Our Access

"It came to pass, while He blessed them, that He was parted from them and carried up into heaven."   —LUKE 24:51

We have no experiences in our lives that correspond to the events in our Lord's life after the transfiguration. From that moment forward His life was altogether substitutionary. Up to the time of the transfiguration, He had exhibited the normal, perfect life of a man. But from the transfiguration forward—Gethsemane, the Cross, the resurrection—everything is unfamiliar to us. His Cross is the door by which every member of the human race can enter into the life of God; by His resurrection He has the right to give eternal life to anyone, and by His ascension our Lord entered heaven, keeping the door open for humanity.

The transfiguration was completed on the Mount of Ascension. If Jesus had gone to heaven directly from the Mount of Transfiguration, He would have gone alone. He would have been nothing more to us than a glorious Figure. But He turned His back on the glory, and came down from the mountain to identify Himself with fallen humanity.

The ascension is the complete fulfillment of the transfiguration. Our Lord returned to His original glory, but not simply as the Son of God—He returned to His Father as the *Son of Man* as well. There is now freedom of access for anyone straight to the very throne of God because of the ascension of the Son of Man. As the Son of Man, Jesus Christ deliberately limited His omnipotence, omnipresence, and omniscience. But now they are His in absolute, full power. As the Son of Man, Jesus Christ now has all the power at the throne of God. From His ascension forward He is the King of kings and Lord of lords.

Lord, how complete and entire and absolute is my need of You in every way and in all ways. Fill me to overflowing with Your glory and beauty.

～ DAY 43 ～

Living Simply—Yet Focused

"Look at the birds of the air . . . . Consider the lilies of the field . . . ."
—MATTHEW 6:26, 28

Consider the lilies of the field, how they grow: they neither toil nor spin"—they simply *are*! Think of the sea, the air, the sun, the stars, and the moon—all of these simply *are* as well—yet what a ministry and service they render on our behalf! So often we impair God's designed influence, which He desires to exhibit through us, because of our own conscious efforts to be consistent and useful. Jesus said there is only one way to develop and grow spiritually, and that is through focusing and concentrating on God. In essence, Jesus was saying, "Do not worry about being of use to others; simply believe on Me." In other words, pay attention to the Source, and out of you "will flow rivers of living water" (John 7:38). We cannot discover the source of our natural life through common sense and reasoning, and Jesus is teaching here that growth in our spiritual life comes not from focusing directly on it, but from concentrating on our Father in heaven. Our heavenly Father knows our circumstances, and if we will stay focused on Him, instead of our circumstances, we will grow spiritually—just as "the lilies of the field."

The people who influence us the most are not those who detain us with their continual talk, but those who live their lives like the stars in the sky and "the lilies of the field"—simply and unaffectedly. Those are the lives that mold and shape us.

If you want to be of use to God, maintain the proper relationship with Jesus Christ by staying focused on Him, and He will make use of you every minute you live—yet you will be unaware, on the conscious level of your life, that you are being used of Him.

I praise You, O Lord, for Your gift of salvation. I thank You for the benefit and blessing of the prayers of Your saints. But, oh, how I slowly begin to think I merit Your favors, or act as though I do. Forgive me, Lord.

∾ DAY 44 ∾

"Out of the Wreck I Rise"

"Who shall separate us from the love of Christ?" ·

—ROMANS 8:35

God does not keep His child immune from trouble; He promises, "I will be with him in trouble . . ." (Psalm 91:15). It doesn't matter how real or intense the adversities may be; nothing can ever separate him from his relationship to God. *"In all these things we are more than conquerors . . ."* (Romans 8:37). Paul was not referring here to imaginary things, but to things that are dangerously real. And he said we are "super-victors" in the midst of them, not because of our own ingenuity, nor because of our courage, but because none of them affects our essential relationship with God in Jesus Christ. I feel sorry for the Christian who doesn't have something in the circumstances of his life that he wishes were not there.

"Shall tribulation . . . ?" Tribulation is never a grand, highly welcomed event; but whatever it may be—whether exhausting, irritating, or simply causing some weakness—it is not able to "separate us from the love of Christ." Never allow tribulations or the "cares of this world" to separate you from remembering that God loves you (Matthew 13:22).

"Shall . . . distress . . . ?" Can God's love continue to hold fast, even when everyone and everything around us seems to be saying that His love is a lie, and that there is no such thing as justice?

"Shall . . . famine . . . ?" Can we not only believe in the love of God but also be "more than conquerors," even while we are being starved?

Either Jesus Christ is a deceiver, having deceived even Paul, or else some extraordinary thing happens to someone who holds on to the love of God when the odds are totally against him. Logic is silenced in the face of each of these things which come against him. Only one thing can account for it—the *love of God in Christ Jesus.* "Out of the wreck I rise" every time.

Lord, I praise You for this place I am in; but the wonder has begun to stir in me—is this Your place for me? Hold me steady doing Your will. It may be only restlessness; if so, calm me to strength that I sin not against You by doubting.

Taking Possession of Our Own Soul

"By your patience possess your souls." —LUKE 21:19

When a person is born again, there is a period of time when he does not have the same vitality in his thinking or reasoning that he previously had. We must learn to express this new life within us, which comes by forming the mind of Christ (see Philippians 2:5). Luke 21:19 means that we take possession of our souls through patience. But many of us prefer to stay at the entrance to the Christian life, instead of going on to create and build our soul in accordance with the new life God has placed within us. We fail because we are ignorant of the way God has made us, and we blame things on the devil that are actually the result of our own undisciplined natures. Just think what we could be when we are awakened to the truth!

There are certain things in life that we need not pray about—moods, for instance. We will never get rid of moodiness by praying, but we will by kicking it out of our lives. Moods nearly always are rooted in some physical circumstance, not in our true inner self. It is a continual struggle not to listen to the moods which arise as a result of our physical condition, but we must never submit to them for a second. We have to pick ourselves up by the back of the neck and shake ourselves; then we will find that we can do what we believed we were unable to do. The problem that most of us are cursed with is simply that we *won't.* The Christian life is one of spiritual courage and determination lived out in our flesh.

Lord, I praise You for Your word—"By your patience possess your souls," and I praise You for Your grace which waits while I laboriously acquire the soul You would have me acquire.

⮜ DAY 46 ⮞

Having God's "Unreasonable" Faith

"Seek first the kingdom of God and His righteousness, and all these things shall be added to you." —MATTHEW 6:33

When we look at these words of Jesus, we immediately find them to be the most revolutionary that human ears have ever heard. "Seek *first* the kingdom of God . . . ." Even the most spiritually-minded of us argue the exact opposite, saying, "But I *must* live; I *must* make a certain amount of money; I *must* be clothed; I *must* be fed." The great concern of our lives is not the kingdom of God but how we are going to take care of ourselves to live. Jesus reversed the order by telling us to get the right relationship with God first, maintaining it as the primary concern of our lives, and never to place our concern on taking care of the other things of life.

"*. . . do not worry about your life . . .*" (6:25). Our Lord pointed out that from His standpoint it is absolutely unreasonable for us to be anxious, worrying about how we will live. Jesus did not say that the person who takes no thought for anything in his life is blessed—no, that person is a fool. But Jesus *did* teach that His disciple must make his relationship with God the dominating focus of his life, and to be cautiously carefree about everything else in comparison to that. In essence, Jesus was saying, "Don't make food and drink the controlling factor of your life, but be focused absolutely on God." Some people are careless about what they eat and drink, and they suffer for it; they are careless about what they wear, having no business looking the way they do; they are careless with their earthly matters, and God holds them responsible. Jesus is saying that the greatest concern of life is to place our relationship with God first, and everything else second.

It is one of the most difficult, yet critical, disciplines of the Christian life to allow the Holy Spirit to bring us into absolute harmony with the teaching of Jesus in these verses.

O Lord, flood me with Your grace and glory so that the ample tide of Yourself may be all in all to me.

The Explanation for Our Difficulties

". . . that they all may be one, as You, Father, are in Me, and I in You; that they also may be one in Us . . . ." —JOHN 17:21

If you are going through a time of isolation, seemingly all alone, read John 17. It will explain exactly why you are where you are—because Jesus has prayed that you "may be one" with the Father as He is. Are you helping God to answer that prayer, or do you have some other goal for your life? Since you became a disciple, you cannot be as independent as you used to be.

God reveals in John 17 that His purpose is not just to answer our prayers, but that through prayer we might come to discern His mind. Yet there is one prayer which God must answer, and that is the prayer of Jesus—". . . that they may be one just as We are one . . ." (17:22). Are we as close to Jesus Christ as that?

God is not concerned about our plans; He doesn't ask, "Do you want to go through this loss of a loved one, this difficulty, or this defeat?" No, He allows these things for His own purpose. The things we are going through are either making us sweeter, better, and nobler men and women, or they are making us more critical and faultfinding, and more insistent on our own way. The things that happen either make us evil, or they make us more saintly, depending entirely on our relationship with God and its level of intimacy. If we will pray, regarding our own lives, "Your will be done" (Matthew 26:42), then we will be encouraged and comforted by John 17, knowing that our Father is working according to His own wisdom, accomplishing what is best. When we understand God's purpose, we will not become small-minded and cynical.

Jesus prayed nothing less for us than absolute oneness with Himself, just as He was one with the Father. Some of us are far from this oneness; yet God will not leave us alone until we *are* one with Him—because Jesus prayed, ". . . that they *all* may be one . . . ."

How helpless I am in bringing forth fruit—Your kind of fruit in the world—so ungenerous and unlike You am I. Forgive me, and by abiding in Jesus may I bear much fruit and so glorify the Father.

∼ DAY 48 ∼

"The Secret of the Lord"

"The secret of the Lord is with those who fear Him . . . ."
—PSALM 25:14

What is the sign of a friend? Is it that he tells you his secret sorrows? No, it is that he tells you his secret joys. Many people will confide their secret sorrows to you, but the final mark of intimacy is when they share their secret joys with you. Have we ever let God tell us any of His joys? Or are we continually telling God our secrets, leaving Him no time to talk to us? At the beginning of our Christian life we are full of requests to God. But then we find that God wants to get us into an intimate relationship with Himself—to get us in touch with His purposes. Are we so intimately united to Jesus Christ's idea of prayer—"Your will be done" (Matthew 6:10)—that we catch the secrets of God? What makes God so dear to us is not so much His big blessings to us, but the tiny things, because they show His amazing intimacy with us—He knows every detail of each of our individual lives.

"Him shall He teach in the way He chooses" (Psalm 25:12). At first, we want the awareness of being guided by God. But then as we grow spiritually, we live so fully aware of God that we do not even need to ask what His will is, because the thought of choosing another way will never occur to us. If we are saved and sanctified, God guides us by our everyday choices. And if we are about to choose what He does not want, He will give us a sense of doubt or restraint, which we must heed. Whenever there is doubt, stop at once. Never try to reason it out, saying, "I wonder why I shouldn't do this?" God instructs us in what we choose; that is, He actually guides our common sense. And when we yield to His teachings and guidance, we no longer hinder His Spirit by continually asking, "Now, Lord, what is Your will?"

O Lord, how wholesome and grand a thing it is to be willing toward You. I am willing, eagerly willing for Your will to be done, and I feel deeply joyful at the prospect, for nothing can be so glorious as just Your will.

⮌ DAY 49 ⮎

The Never-Forsaking God

"He Himself has said, 'I will never leave you nor forsake you.'"
—HEBREWS 13:5

What line of thinking do my thoughts take? Do I turn to what God says or to my own fears? Am I simply repeating what God says, or am I learning to truly hear Him and then to respond after I have heard what He says? "For He Himself has said, 'I will never leave you nor forsake you.' So we may boldly say: 'The Lord is my helper; I will not fear. What can man do to me?'" (13:5–6).

"I will never leave you . . ."—not for any reason; not my sin, selfishness, stubbornness, nor waywardness. Have I really let God say to me that He will never leave me? If I have not truly heard this assurance of God, then let me listen again.

"I will never . . . forsake you." Sometimes it is not the difficulty of life but the drudgery of it that makes me think God will forsake me. When there is no major difficulty to overcome, no vision from God, nothing wonderful or beautiful—just the everyday activities of life—do I hear God's assurance even in these?

We have the idea that God is going to do some exceptional thing— that He is preparing and equipping us for some extraordinary work in the future. But as we grow in His grace we find that God is glorifying Himself here and now, at this very moment. If we have God's assurance behind us, the most amazing strength becomes ours, and we learn to sing, glorifying Him even in the ordinary days and ways of life.

O Lord, rise in grandeur into my life and ways and goings. Be a strong presence of healing and hope and grace and beauty this day.

⤙ DAY 50 ⤚

God's Assurance

"He Himself has said . . . . So we may boldly say . . . ."
—HEBREWS 13:5–6

My assurance is to be built upon God's assurance to me. God says, "I will never leave you," so that then I "may boldly say, 'The Lord is my helper; I will not fear'" (13:5–6). In other words, I will not be obsessed with apprehension. This does not mean that I will not be tempted to fear, but I will remember God's words of assurance. I will be full of courage, like a child who strives to reach the standard his father has set for him. The faith of many people begins to falter when apprehensions enter their thinking, and they forget the meaning of God's assurance—they forget to take a deep spiritual breath. The only way to remove the fear from our lives is to listen to God's assurance to us.

What are you fearing? Whatever it may be, you are not a coward about it—you are determined to face it, yet you still have a feeling of fear. When it seems that there is nothing and no one to help you, say to yourself, "But 'The Lord is my helper' this very moment, even in my present circumstance." Are you learning to listen to God before you speak, or are you saying things and then trying to make God's Word fit what you have said? Take hold of the Father's assurance, and then say with strong courage, "I will not fear." It does not matter what evil or wrong may be in our way, because "He Himself has said, 'I will never leave you . . . .'"

Human frailty is another thing that gets between God's words of assurance and our own words and thoughts. When we realize how feeble we are in facing difficulties, the difficulties become like giants, we become like grasshoppers, and God seems to be nonexistent. But remember God's assurance to us—*"I will never . . . forsake you."* Have we learned to sing after hearing God's keynote? Are we continually filled with enough courage to say, "The Lord is my helper," or are we yielding to fear?

O Lord, speak to me now. Inspire me for today. Be my helper against the dullness, deep and devastating, that seems to hold fast to my powers.

"Work Out" What God "Works In" You

*". . . work out your own salvation . . . for it is God who works in you
. . . ."* —PHILIPPIANS 2:12–13

Your will agrees with God, but in your flesh there is a nature that renders you powerless to do what you know you ought to do. When the Lord initially comes in contact with our conscience, the first thing our conscience does is awaken our will, and our will always agrees with God. Yet you say, "But I don't know if my will is in agreement with God." Look to Jesus and you will find that your will and your conscience are in agreement with Him every time. What causes you to say "I will not obey" is something less deep and penetrating than your will. It is perversity or stubbornness, and they are never in agreement with God. The most profound thing in a person is his will, not sin.

The will is the essential element in God's creation of human beings— sin is a perverse nature which entered into people. In someone who has been born again, the source of the will is Almighty God. ". . . for it is God who works in you both to will and to do for His good pleasure." With focused attention and great care, you have to "work out" what God "works in" you—not *work* to accomplish or earn "your own salvation," but *work it out* so you will exhibit the evidence of a life based with determined, unshakable faith on the complete and perfect redemption of the Lord. As you do this, you do not bring an opposing will up against God's will— God's will *is* your will. Your natural choices will be in accordance with God's will, and living this life will be as natural as breathing. Stubbornness is an unintelligent barrier, refusing enlightenment and blocking its flow. The only thing to do with this barrier of stubbornness is to blow it up with "dynamite," and the "dynamite" is obedience to the Holy Spirit.

Do I believe that Almighty God is the Source of my will? God not only expects me to do His will, but He is in me to do it.

Lord, lift me as I lift myself up to You. Give me the light of Your countenance that I may radiate it back to You.

The Greatest Source of Power

"Whatever you ask in My name, that I will do . . . ." —JOHN 14:13

A m I fulfilling this ministry of intercession deep within the hidden recesses of my life? There is no trap nor any danger at all of being deceived or of showing pride in true intercession. It is a hidden ministry that brings forth fruit through which the Father is glorified. Am I allowing my spiritual life to waste away, or am I focused, bringing everything to one central point—the atonement of my Lord? Is Jesus Christ more and more dominating every interest of my life? If the central point, or the most powerful influence, of my life is the atonement of the Lord, then every aspect of my life will bear fruit for Him.

However, I must take the time to realize what this central point of power is. Am I willing to give one minute out of every hour to concentrate on it? "If you abide in Me . . . "—that is, if you continue to act, and think, and work from that central point—"you will ask what you desire, and it shall be done for you" (John 15:7). Am I abiding? Am I taking the time to abide? What is the greatest source of power in my life? Is it my work, service, and sacrifice for others, or is it my striving to work for God? It should be none of these—what ought to exert the greatest power in my life is the atonement of the Lord. It is not on what we spend the greatest amount of time that molds us the most, but whatever exerts the most power over us. We must make a determination to limit and concentrate our desires and interests on the atonement by the Cross of Christ.

"Whatever you ask in My name, that I will do . . . ." The disciple who abides in Jesus *is* the will of God, and what appears to be his free choices are actually God's foreordained decrees. Is this mysterious? Does it appear to contradict sound logic or seem totally absurd? Yes, but what a glorious truth it is to a saint of God.

O Lord, I praise You for the Throne of Grace and that in Jesus Christ I can draw near with boldness to receive mercy and grace for this day's glorifying of You.

❧ DAY 53 ❧

What's Next to Do?

"If you know these things, blessed are you if you do them."

—JOHN 13:17

Be determined to know more than others. If you yourself do not cut the lines that tie you to the dock, God will have to use a storm to sever them and to send you out to sea. Put everything in your life afloat upon God, going out to sea on the great swelling tide of His purpose, and your eyes will be opened. If you believe in Jesus, you are not to spend all your time in the calm waters just inside the harbor, full of joy, but always tied to the dock. You have to get out past the harbor into the great depths of God, and begin to know things for yourself—begin to have spiritual discernment.

When you know that you should do something and you do it, immediately you know more. Examine where you have become sluggish, where you began losing interest spiritually, and you will find that it goes back to a point where you did not do something you knew you should do. You did not do it because there seemed to be no immediate call to do it. But now you have no insight or discernment, and at a time of crisis you are spiritually distracted instead of spiritually self-controlled. It is a dangerous thing to refuse to continue learning and knowing more.

The counterfeit of obedience is a state of mind in which you create your own opportunities to sacrifice yourself, and your zeal and enthusiasm are mistaken for discernment. It is easier to sacrifice yourself than to fulfill your spiritual destiny, which is stated in Romans 12:1–2. It is much better to fulfill the purpose of God in your life by discerning His will than it is to perform great acts of self-sacrifice. "Behold, to obey is better than sacrifice . . ." (1 Samuel 15:22). Beware of paying attention or going back to what you once were, when God wants you to be something that you have never been. "If anyone wills to do His will, he shall know . . ." (John 7:17).

Lord, bring me closer and closer to You until I am more and more useful to You in Your enterprises.

⁊ DAY 54 ⁊
Then What's Next to Do?

"Everyone who asks receives . . . ."   —LUKE 11:10

Ask if you have not received. There is nothing more difficult than asking. We will have yearnings and desires for certain things, and even suffer as a result of their going unfulfilled, but not until we are at the limit of desperation will we *ask*. It is the sense of not being spiritually real that causes us to ask. Have you ever asked out of the depths of your total insufficiency and poverty? "If any of you lacks wisdom, let him ask of God . . ." (James 1:5), but be sure that you do lack wisdom before you ask. You cannot bring yourself to the point of spiritual reality anytime you choose. The best thing to do, once you realize you are not spiritually real, is to ask God for the Holy Spirit, basing your request on the promise of Jesus Christ (see Luke 11:13). The Holy Spirit is the one who makes everything that Jesus did for you real in your life.

"Everyone who asks receives . . . ." This does not mean that you will not *get* if you do not ask, but it means that until you come to the point of asking, you will not *receive* from God (see Matthew 5:45). To be able to receive means that you have to come into the relationship of a child of God, and then you comprehend and appreciate mentally, morally, and with spiritual understanding, that these things come from God.

"If any of you lacks wisdom . . . ." If you realize that you are lacking, it is because you have come in contact with spiritual reality—do not put the blinders of reason on again. The word *ask* actually means "beg." Some people are poor enough to be interested in their poverty, and some of us are poor enough spiritually to show our interest. Yet we will never receive if we ask with a certain result in mind, because we are asking out of our lust, not out of our poverty. A pauper does not ask out of any reason other than the completely hopeless and painful condition of his poverty. He is not ashamed to beg—blessed are the *paupers* in spirit (see Matthew 5:3).

It is all so mysterious, O Lord, and all so simple—I pray and believe that You create something in answer to, and by the very means of, my prayer that was not in existence before. Thank You.

And After That What's Next to Do?

". . . seek, and you will find . . . ." —LUKE 11:9

Seek if you have not found. "You ask and do not receive, because you ask amiss . . ." (James 4:3). If you ask for things from life instead of from God, "you ask amiss"; that is, you ask out of your desire for self-fulfillment. The more you fulfill yourself the less you will seek God. ". . . seek, and you will find . . . ." Get to work—narrow your focus and interests to this one thing. Have you ever sought God with your whole heart, or have you simply given Him a feeble cry after some emotionally painful experience? ". . . seek, [focus,] and you will find . . . ."

"Ho! Everyone who thirsts, come to the waters. . ." (Isaiah 55:1). Are you thirsty, or complacent and indifferent—so satisfied with your own experience that you want nothing more of God? Experience is a doorway, not a final goal. Beware of building your faith on experience, or your life will not ring true and will only sound the note of a critical spirit. Remember that you can never give another person what you have found, but you can cause him to have a desire for it.

". . . knock, and it will be opened to you" (Luke 11:9). "Draw near to God . . ." (James 4:8). Knock—the door is closed, and your heartbeat races as you knock. "Cleanse your hands . . ." (4:8). Knock a bit louder—you begin to find that you are dirty. ". . . purify your hearts . . ." (4:8). It is becoming even more personal—you are desperate and serious now—you will do anything. "Lament . . . " (4:9). Have you ever lamented, expressing your sorrow before God for the condition of your inner life? There is no thread of self-pity left, only the heartrending difficulty and amazement which comes from seeing what kind of person you really are. "Humble yourselves . . . " (4:10). It is a humbling experience to knock at God's door—you have to knock with the crucified thief. ". . . to him who knocks *it will be opened*" (Luke 11:10).

O Lord, I would that I had a livelier sense of You and of Your bounties continually with me.

❧ DAY 56 ❧

Getting There

"Come to Me . . . ."   —MATTHEW 11:28

Where sin and sorrow stops, and the song of the saint starts. Do I really want to get there? I can right now. The questions that truly matter in life are remarkably few, and they are all answered by these words—"Come to Me." Our Lord's words are not, "Do this, or don't do that," but—"Come to Me." If I will simply come to Jesus, my real life will be brought into harmony with my real desires. I will actually cease from sin, and will find the song of the Lord beginning in my life.

Have you ever come to Jesus? Look at the stubbornness of your heart. You would rather do anything than this one simple childlike thing—"Come to Me." If you really want to experience ceasing from sin, you must come to Jesus.

Jesus Christ makes Himself the test to determine your genuineness. Look how He used the word *come*. At the most unexpected moments in your life there is this whisper of the Lord—"Come to Me," and you are immediately drawn to Him. Personal contact with Jesus changes everything. Be "foolish" enough to come and commit yourself to what He says. The attitude necessary for you to come to Him is one where your will has made the determination to let go of everything and deliberately commit it all to Him.

". . . and I will give you rest"—that is, "I will sustain you, causing you to stand firm." He is not saying, "I will put you to bed, hold your hand, and sing you to sleep." But, in essence, He is saying, "I will get you out of bed—out of your listlessness and exhaustion, and out of your condition of being half dead while you are still alive. I will penetrate you with the spirit of life, and you will be sustained by the perfection of vital activity." Yet we become so weak and pitiful and talk about "suffering" the will of the Lord! Where is the majestic vitality and the power of the Son of God in that?

"Like rain upon the mown grass" . . . "as the dew unto Israel"—O Lord, these phrases come to my mind this morning with sweet insistence. Be as rain and as dew unto us this day, refreshing, remolding, and blessing us. Unto You do I come in great and glad expectancy.

Getting There

"They said to Him, 'Rabbi . . . where are You staying?' He said to them, 'Come and see.'" —JOHN 1:38–39

Where our self-interest sleeps and the real interest is awakened. "They . . . remained with Him that day . . . ." That is about all some of us ever do. We stay with Him a short time, only to wake up to our own realities of life. Our self-interest rises up and our abiding with Him is past. Yet there is no circumstance of life in which we cannot abide in Jesus.

"You are Simon . . . . You shall be called Cephas" (1:42). God writes our new name only on those places in our lives where He has erased our pride, self-sufficiency, and self-interest. Some of us have our new name written only in certain spots, like spiritual measles. And in those areas of our lives we look all right. When we are in our best spiritual mood, you would think we were the highest quality saints. But don't dare look at us when we are not in that mood. A true disciple is one who has his new name written all over him— self-interest, pride, and self-sufficiency have been completely erased.

Pride is the sin of making "self" our god. And some of us today do this, not like the Pharisee, but like the tax collector (see Luke 18:9–14). For you to say, "Oh, I'm no saint," is acceptable by human standards of pride, but it is unconscious blasphemy against God. You defy God to make you a saint, as if to say, "I am too weak and hopeless and outside the reach of the atonement by the Cross of Christ." Why aren't you a saint? It is either that you do not want to be a saint, or that you do not believe that God can make you into one. You say it would be all right if God saved you and took you straight to heaven. That is exactly what He will do! And not only do we make our home with Him, but Jesus said of His Father and Himself, ". . . We will come to him and make Our home with him" (John 14:23). Put no conditions on your life—let Jesus be everything to you, and He will take you home with Him not only for a day, but for eternity.

O Lord, how much the margins of my mind are taken up with surrounding interests of late so that the surroundings seem the center. O Lord, may You be my strong Center and Surrounding.

❧ DAY 58 ❧

Getting There

". . . come, follow Me." —LUKE 18:22

Where our individual desire dies and sanctified surrender lives. One of the greatest hindrances in coming to Jesus is the excuse of our own individual temperament. We make our temperament and our natural desires barriers to coming to Jesus. Yet the first thing we realize when we do come to Jesus is that He pays no attention whatsoever to our natural desires. We have the idea that we can dedicate our gifts to God. However, you cannot dedicate what is not yours. There is actually only one thing you can dedicate to God, and that is your right to yourself (see Romans 12:1). If you will give God your right to yourself, He will make a holy experiment out of you—and His experiments always succeed. The one true mark of a saint of God is the inner creativity that flows from being totally surrendered to Jesus Christ. In the life of a saint there is this amazing Well, which is a continual Source of original life. The Spirit of God is a Well of water springing up perpetually fresh. A saint realizes that it is God who engineers his circumstances; consequently there are no complaints, only unrestrained surrender to Jesus. Never try to make your experience a principle for others, but allow God to be as creative and original with others as He is with you.

If you abandon everything to Jesus, and come when He says, "Come," then He will continue to say, "Come," through you. You will go out into the world reproducing the echo of Christ's "Come." That is the result in every soul who has abandoned all and come to Jesus.

Have I come to Him? Will I come *now*?

O Lord, what great and glorious plans You have for us. Lord, we do not see the way, but we know You and trust. Keep our minds and hearts strong and quiet in You.

⌒ DAY 59 ⌒

Get Moving!

"Abide in Me . . . ."   —JOHN 15:4

In the matter of determination. The Spirit of Jesus is put into me by way of the atonement by the Cross of Christ. I then have to build my thinking patiently to bring it into perfect harmony with my Lord. God will not make me think like Jesus—I have to do it myself. I have to bring "every thought into captivity to the obedience of Christ" (2 Corinthians 10:5). "Abide in Me"—in intellectual matters, in money matters, in every one of the matters that make human life what it is. Our lives are not made up of only one neatly confined area.

Am I preventing God from doing things in my circumstances by saying that it will only serve to hinder my fellowship with Him? How irrelevant and disrespectful that is! It does not matter what my circumstances are. I can be as much assured of abiding in Jesus in any one of them as I am in any prayer meeting. It is unnecessary to change and arrange my circumstances myself. Our Lord's inner abiding was pure and unblemished. He was at home with God wherever His body was. He never chose His own circumstances, but was meek, submitting to His Father's plans and directions for Him. Just think of how amazingly relaxed our Lord's life was! But we tend to keep God at a fever pitch in our lives. We have none of the serenity of the life which is "hidden with Christ in God" (Colossians 3:3).

Think of the things that take you out of the position of abiding in Christ. You say, "Yes, Lord, just a minute—I still have this to do. Yes, I will abide as soon as this is finished, or as soon as this week is over. It will be all right, Lord. I will abide then." *Get moving*—begin to abide *now*. In the initial stages it will be a continual effort to abide, but as you continue, it will become so much a part of your life that you will abide in Him without any conscious effort. Make the determination to abide in Jesus wherever you are now or wherever you may be placed in the future.

O Lord, I come to You with praise and thanksgiving, but with a yearning for a deeper conscious appreciation of Your goodness. Bless me this day with an enlarged capacity and power to praise.

⚘ DAY 60 ⚘

Get Moving!

"Also . . . add to your faith . . . ."   —2 PETER 1:5

In the matter of drudgery. Peter said in this passage that we have become "partakers of the divine nature" and that we should now be "giving all diligence," concentrating on forming godly habits (1:4–5). We are to "add" to our lives all that character means. No one is born either naturally or supernaturally with character; it must be developed. Nor are we born with habits—we have to form godly habits on the basis of the new life God has placed within us. We are not meant to be seen as God's perfect, bright-shining examples, but to be seen as the everyday essence of ordinary life exhibiting the miracle of His grace. Drudgery is the test of genuine character. The greatest hindrance in our spiritual life is that we will only look for big things to do. Yet, "Jesus . . . took a towel and . . . began to wash the disciples' feet . . ." (John 13:3–5).

We all have those times when there are no flashes of light and no apparent thrill to life, where we experience nothing but the daily routine with its common everyday tasks. The routine of life is actually God's way of saving us between our times of great inspiration which come from Him. Don't always expect God to give you His thrilling moments, but learn to live in those common times of the drudgery of life by the power of God.

It is difficult for us to do the "adding" that Peter mentioned here. We say we do not expect God to take us to heaven on flowery beds of ease, and yet we act as if we do! I must realize that my obedience even in the smallest detail of life has all of the omnipotent power of the grace of God behind it. If I will do my duty, not for duty's sake but because I believe God is engineering my circumstances, then at the very point of my obedience all of the magnificent grace of God is mine through the glorious atonement by the Cross of Christ.

O Lord, how slow is my growth in Your almighty grace! Open my nature to grander horizons this day.

⬿ DAY 61 ⬾

Receiving Yourself in
the Fires of Sorrow

*". . . what shall I say? 'Father, save Me from this hour'? But for this pur-
pose I came to this hour. 'Father, glorify Your name.'"*

—JOHN 12:27–28

As a saint of God, my attitude toward sorrow and difficulty should not
be to ask that they be prevented, but to ask that God protect me so
that I may remain what He created me to be, in spite of all my fires of sorrow. Our Lord received Himself, accepting His position and realizing His
purpose, in the midst of the fire of sorrow. He was saved not *from* the hour,
but *out of* the hour.

We say that there ought to be no sorrow, but there *is* sorrow, and we have
to accept and receive ourselves in its fires. If we try to evade sorrow, refusing
to deal with it, we are foolish. Sorrow is one of the biggest facts in life, and
there is no use in saying it should not be. Sin, sorrow, and suffering *are*, and
it is not for us to say that God has made a mistake in allowing them.

Sorrow removes a great deal of a person's shallowness, but it does not
always make that person better. Suffering either gives me to myself or it
destroys me. You cannot find or receive yourself through success, because
you lose your head over pride. And you cannot receive yourself through the
monotony of your daily life, because you give in to complaining. The only
way to find yourself is in the fires of sorrow. Why it should be this way is
immaterial. The fact is that it is true in the Scriptures and in human experience. You can always recognize who has been through the fires of sorrow
and received himself, and you know that you can go to him in your moment
of trouble and find that he has plenty of time for you. But if a person has not
been through the fires of sorrow, he is apt to be contemptuous, having no
respect or time for you, only turning you away. If you will receive yourself in
the fires of sorrow, God will make you nourishment for other people.

---

*Lord, cause Your loving-kindness to be known by me this day by Your inevitably
powerful touches, and use me in Your gentle almightiness for Your purposes.*

Drawing on the Grace of God—Now

"We . . . plead with you not to receive the grace of God in vain."
—2 CORINTHIANS 6:1

The grace you had yesterday will not be sufficient for today. Grace is the overflowing favor of God, and you can always count on it being available to draw upon as needed. ". . . in much patience, in tribulations, in needs, in distresses"—that is where our patience is tested (6:4). Are you failing to rely on the grace of God there? Are you saying to yourself, "Oh well, I won't count this time"? It is not a question of praying and asking God to help you—it is taking the grace of God *now*. We tend to make prayer the preparation for our service, yet it is never that in the Bible. Prayer is the practice of drawing on the grace of God. Don't say, "I will endure this until I can get away and pray." Pray *now*—draw on the grace of God in your moment of need. Prayer is the most normal and useful thing; it is not simply a reflex action of your devotion to God. We are very slow to learn to draw on God's grace through prayer.

". . . in stripes, in imprisonments, in tumults, in labors . . ." (6:5)—in all these things, display in your life a drawing on the grace of God, which will show evidence to yourself and to others that you are a miracle of His. Draw on His grace now, not later. The primary word in the spiritual vocabulary is *now*. Let circumstances take you where they will, but keep drawing on the grace of God in whatever condition you may find yourself. One of the greatest proofs that you are drawing on the grace of God is that you can be totally humiliated before others without displaying even the slightest trace of anything but His grace.

". . . having nothing . . . ." Never hold anything in reserve. Pour yourself out, giving the best that you have, and always be poor. Never be diplomatic and careful with the treasure God gives you. ". . . and yet possessing all things"—this is poverty triumphant (6:10).

O Lord, for supplies of Your grace today, grace so divine and mighty that my life and witness may glorify You.

✑ DAY 63 ✎

The Overshadowing of God's
Personal Deliverance

" '. . . I am with you to deliver you,' says the Lord."

—JEREMIAH 1:8

God promised Jeremiah that He would deliver him personally—". . . your life shall be as a prize to you . . ." (Jeremiah 39:18). That is all God promises His children. Wherever God sends us, He will guard our lives. Our personal property and possessions are to be a matter of indifference to us, and our hold on these things should be very loose. If this is not the case, we will have panic, heartache, and distress. Having the proper outlook is evidence of the deeply rooted belief in the overshadowing of God's personal deliverance.

The Sermon on the Mount indicates that when we are on a mission for Jesus Christ, there is no time to stand up for ourselves. Jesus says, in effect, "Don't worry about whether or not you are being treated justly." Looking for justice is actually a sign that we have been diverted from our devotion to Him. Never look for justice in this world, but never cease to give it. If we look for justice, we will only begin to complain and to indulge ourselves in the discontent of self-pity, as if to say, "Why should I be treated like this?" If we are devoted to Jesus Christ, we have nothing to do with what we encounter, whether it is just or unjust. In essence, Jesus says, "Continue steadily on with what I have told you to do, and I will guard your life. If you try to guard it yourself, you remove yourself from My deliverance." Even the most devout among us become atheistic in this regard—we do not believe Him. We put our common sense on the throne and then attach God's name to it. We *do* lean to our own understanding, instead of trusting God with all our hearts (see Proverbs 3:5–6).

———

O Lord, I know Your blessing and I praise You, but it is the indescribable touch and encircling as Your servant that I seek for—I know not what I seek for, but You know. How I long for You!

ᗕ DAY 64 ᗒ
Held by the Grip of God

"I press on, that I may lay hold of that for which Christ Jesus has also laid hold of me." —PHILIPPIANS 3:12

Never choose to be a worker for God, but once God has placed His call on you, woe be to you if you "turn aside to the right hand or to the left" (Deuteronomy 5:32). We are not here to work for God because we have chosen to do so, but because God has "laid hold of" us. And once He has done so, we never have this thought, "Well, I'm really not suited for this." What you are to preach is also determined by God, not by your own natural leanings or desires. Keep your soul steadfastly related to God, and remember that you are called not simply to convey your testimony but also to preach the gospel. Every Christian must testify to the truth of God, but when it comes to the call to preach, there must be the agonizing grip of God's hand on you—your life is in the grip of God for that very purpose. How many of us are held like that?

Never water down the Word of God, but preach it in its undiluted sternness. There must be unflinching faithfulness to the Word of God, but when you come to personal dealings with others, remember who you are—you are not some special being created in heaven, but a sinner saved by grace.

"Brethren, I do not count myself to have apprehended; but *one thing I do* . . . I press toward the goal for the prize of the upward call of God in Christ Jesus" (Philippians 3:13–14).

Lord, that I might see You, feel You, and fully realize You in the manner and measure You see I am capable of. What wait I for but You only?

⸙ DAY 65 ⸙

The Strictest Discipline

"If your right hand causes you to sin, cut it off and cast it from you; for it is more profitable for you that one of your members perish, than for your whole body to be cast into hell." —MATTHEW 5:30

Jesus did not say that everyone must cut off his right hand, but that "if your right hand causes you to sin" in your walk with Him, then it is better to "cut it off." There are many things that are perfectly legitimate, but if you are going to concentrate on God you cannot do them. Your right hand is one of the best things you have, but Jesus says that if it hinders you in following His precepts, then "cut it off." The principle taught here is the strictest discipline or lesson that ever hit humankind.

When God changes you through regeneration, giving you new life through spiritual rebirth, your life initially has the characteristic of being maimed. There are a hundred and one things that you dare not do—things that would be sin for you, and would be recognized as sin by those who really know you. But the unspiritual people around you will say, "What's so wrong with doing that? How absurd you are!" There has never yet been a saint who has not lived a maimed life initially. Yet it is better to enter into life maimed but lovely in God's sight than to appear lovely to man's eyes but lame to God's. At first, Jesus Christ through His Spirit has to restrain you from doing a great many things that may be perfectly right for everyone else but not right for you. Yet, see that you don't use your restrictions to criticize someone else.

The Christian life is a maimed life initially, but in verse 48 Jesus gave us the picture of a perfectly well-rounded life—"You shall be *perfect*, just as your Father in heaven is perfect."

O Lord, this day lead me into some more of Your gracious and wondrous doings. Put Your loving hand of grace and power upon me this day.

⁓ DAY 66 ⁓

Do It Now!

"Agree with your adversary quickly . . . ."   —MATTHEW 5:25

In this verse, Jesus Christ laid down a very important principle by saying, "Do what you know you must do—*now*. Do it quickly. If you don't, an inevitable process will begin to work 'till you have paid the last penny' (5:26) in pain, agony, and distress." God's laws are unchangeable and there is no escape from them. The teachings of Jesus always penetrate right to the heart of our being.

Wanting to make sure that my adversary gives me all my rights is a natural thing. But Jesus says that it is a matter of inescapable and eternal importance to me that I pay my adversary what I owe him. From our Lord's standpoint it doesn't matter whether I am cheated or not, but what does matter is that I don't cheat someone else. Am I insisting on having my own rights, or am I paying what I owe from Jesus Christ's standpoint?

Do it quickly—bring yourself to judgment now. In moral and spiritual matters, you must act immediately. If you don't, the inevitable, relentless process will begin to work. God is determined to have His child as pure, clean, and white as driven snow, and as long as there is disobedience in any point of His teaching, He will allow His Spirit to use whatever process it may take to bring us to obedience. The fact that we insist on proving that we are right is almost always a clear indication that we have some point of disobedience. No wonder the Spirit of God so strongly urges us to stay steadfastly in the light (see John 3:19–21)!

"Agree with your adversary quickly . . . ." Have you suddenly reached a certain place in your relationship with someone, only to find that you have anger in your heart? Confess it quickly—make it right before God. Be reconciled to that person—*do it now!*

Lord, be unto me a place of broad rivers, full of life and restful activity. Show forth Your love and gentleness in me today, and through me to those who are influenced directly by me.

≈ DAY 67 ≈

"You Are Not Your Own"

"Do you not know that . . . you are not your own?"
—1 CORINTHIANS 6:19

There is no such thing as a private life, or a place to hide in this world, for a man or woman who is intimately aware of and shares in the sufferings of Jesus Christ. God divides the private life of His saints and makes it a highway for the world on one hand and for Himself on the other. No human being can stand that unless he is identified with Jesus Christ. We are not sanctified for ourselves. We are called into intimacy with the gospel, and things happen that appear to have nothing to do with us. But God is getting us into fellowship with Himself. Let Him have His way. If you refuse, you will be of no value to God in His redemptive work in the world, but will be a hindrance and a stumbling block.

The first thing God does is get us grounded on strong reality and truth. He does this until our cares for ourselves individually have been brought into submission to His way for the purpose of His redemption. Why shouldn't we experience heartbreak? Through those doorways God is opening up ways of fellowship with His Son. Most of us collapse at the first grip of pain. We sit down at the door of God's purpose and enter a slow death through self-pity. And all the so-called Christian sympathy of others helps us to our deathbed. But God will not. He comes with the grip of the pierced hand of His Son, as if to say, "Enter into fellowship with Me; arise and shine." If God can accomplish His purposes in this world through a broken heart, then why not thank Him for breaking yours?

O Lord, speak with power and graciousness today. Conduct me into the inner secret of fellowship with You that You may be able to convey Yourself aright.

⊱ DAY 68 ⊰

Obedience or Independence?

"If you love Me, keep My commandments." —JOHN 14:15

Our Lord never insists on our obedience. He stresses very definitely what we *ought* to do, but He never *forces* us to do it. We have to obey Him out of a oneness of spirit with Him. That is why whenever our Lord talked about discipleship, He prefaced it with an "If," meaning, "You do not need to do this unless you desire to do so." "*If* anyone desires to come after Me, let him deny himself . . ." (Luke 9:23). In other words, "To be My disciple, let him give up his right to himself to Me." Our Lord is not talking about our eternal position, but about our being of value to Him in this life here and now. That is why He sounds so stern (see Luke 14:26). Never try to make sense from these words by separating them from the One who spoke them.

The Lord does not give me rules, but He makes His standard very clear. If my relationship to Him is that of love, I will do what He says without hesitation. If I hesitate, it is because I love someone I have placed in competition with Him, namely, myself. Jesus Christ will not force me to obey Him, but I must. And as soon as I obey Him, I fulfill my spiritual destiny. My personal life may be crowded with small, petty happenings, altogether insignificant. But if I obey Jesus Christ in the seemingly random circumstances of life, they become pinholes through which I see the face of God. Then, when I stand face to face with God, I will discover that through my obedience thousands were blessed. When God's redemption brings a human soul to the point of obedience, it always produces. If I obey Jesus Christ, the redemption of God will flow through me to the lives of others, because behind the deed of obedience is the reality of Almighty God.

O Lord, explore down to the deepest springs of my spirit where the Spirit makes intercession for us and reads prayers I cannot utter.

A Bondservant of Jesus

"I have been crucified with Christ; it is no longer I who live, but Christ lives in me . . . ." —GALATIANS 2:20

These words mean the breaking and collapse of my independence brought about by my own hands, and the surrendering of my life to the supremacy of the Lord Jesus. No one can do this for me, I must do it myself. God may bring me up to this point three hundred and sixty-five times a year, but He cannot push me through it. It means breaking the hard outer layer of my individual independence from God, and the liberating of myself and my nature into oneness with Him; not following my own ideas, but choosing absolute loyalty to Jesus. Once I am at that point, there is no possibility of misunderstanding. Very few of us know anything about loyalty to Christ or understand what He meant when He said, *". . . for My sake"* (Matthew 5:11). That is what makes a strong saint.

Has that breaking of my independence come? All the rest is religious fraud. The one point to decide is—will I give up? Will I surrender to Jesus Christ, placing no conditions whatsoever as to how the brokenness will come? I must be broken from my own understanding of myself. When I reach that point, immediately the reality of the supernatural identification with Jesus Christ takes place. And the witness of the Spirit of God is unmistakable—"I have been crucified with Christ . . . ."

The passion of Christianity comes from deliberately signing away my own rights and becoming a bondservant of Jesus Christ. Until I do that, I will not begin to be a saint.

One student a year who hears God's call would be sufficient for God to have called the Bible Training College into existence. This college has no value as an organization, not even academically. Its sole value for existence is for God to help Himself to lives. Will we allow Him to help Himself to us, or are we more concerned with our own ideas of what we are going to be?

Lord, my approach to You is dulled because of physical dimness, but my heart is glad, and my flesh also shall rest in hope.

∽ DAY 70 ∾
The Authority of Truth

"Draw near to God and He will draw near to you." —JAMES 4:8

It is essential that you give people the opportunity to act on the truth of God. The responsibility must be left with the individual—you cannot act for him. It must be his own deliberate act, but the evangelical message should always lead him to action. Refusing to act leaves a person paralyzed, exactly where he was previously.

But once he acts, he is never the same. It is the apparent folly of the truth that stands in the way of hundreds who have been convicted by the Spirit of God. Once I press myself into action, I immediately begin to live. Anything less is merely existing. The moments I truly live are the moments when I act with my entire will.

When a truth of God is brought home to your soul, never allow it to pass without acting on it internally in your will, not necessarily externally in your physical life. Record it with ink and with blood—work it into your life. The weakest saint who transacts business with Jesus Christ is liberated the second he acts and God's almighty power is available on his behalf. We come up to the truth of God, confess we are wrong, but go back again. Then we approach it again and turn back, until we finally learn we have no business going back. When we are confronted with such a word of truth from our redeeming Lord, we must move directly to transact business with Him. "Come to Me . . ." (Matthew 11:28). His word *come* means "to act." Yet the last thing we want to do is come. But everyone who does come knows that, at that very moment, the supernatural power of the life of God invades him. The dominating power of the world, the flesh, and the devil is now paralyzed; not by your act, but because your act has joined you to God and tapped you in to His redemptive power.

Lord, this one thing—my utterable and unutterable need of You—in entire necessity I come to You. "Poor in spirit" describes my certain knowledge of myself.

⌒ DAY 71 ⌒

Partakers of His Sufferings

". . . but rejoice to the extent that you partake of Christ's sufferings . . . ."
—1 PETER 4:13

If you are going to be used by God, He will take you through a number of experiences that are not meant for you personally at all. They are designed to make you useful in His hands, and to enable you to understand what takes place in the lives of others. Because of this process, you will never be surprised by what comes your way. You say, "Oh, I can't deal with that person." Why can't you? God gave you sufficient opportunities to learn from Him about that problem; but you turned away, not heeding the lesson, because it seemed foolish to spend your time that way.

The sufferings of Christ were not those of ordinary people. He suffered "according to the will of God" (1 Peter 4:19), having a different point of view of suffering from ours. It is only through our relationship with Jesus Christ that we can understand what God is after in His dealings with us. When it comes to suffering, it is part of our Christian culture to want to know God's purpose beforehand. In the history of the Christian church, the tendency has been to avoid being identified with the sufferings of Jesus Christ. People have sought to carry out God's orders through a shortcut of their own. God's way is always the way of suffering—the way of the "long road home."

Are we partakers of Christ's sufferings? Are we prepared for God to stamp out our personal ambitions? Are we prepared for God to destroy our individual decisions by supernaturally transforming them? It will mean not knowing why God is taking us that way, because knowing would make us spiritually proud. We never realize at the time what God is putting us through—we go through it more or less without understanding. Then suddenly we come to a place of enlightenment, and realize—"God has strengthened me and I didn't even know it!"

Lord, for all who are taxed physically, undertake with Your sustaining. Prevent the exacting of the Enemy, and may the joy of the Lord be their strength in a marvelous manner.

⌒ DAY 72 ⌒

Intimate Theology

"Do you believe this?" —JOHN 11:26

Martha believed in the power available to Jesus Christ; she believed that if He had been there He could have healed her brother; she also believed that Jesus had a special intimacy with God, and that whatever He asked of God, God would do. But—she needed a closer personal intimacy with Jesus. Martha's theology had its fulfillment in the future. But Jesus continued to attract and draw her in until her belief became an intimate possession. It then slowly emerged into a personal inheritance—"Yes, Lord, I believe that You are the Christ . . ." (11:27).

Is the Lord dealing with you in the same way? Is Jesus teaching you to have a personal intimacy with Himself? Allow Him to drive His question home to you—"Do you believe *this?*" Are you facing an area of doubt in your life? Have you come, like Martha, to a crossroads of overwhelming circumstances where your theology is about to become a very personal belief? This happens only when a personal problem brings the awareness of our personal need.

To believe is to commit. In the area of intellectual learning I commit myself mentally, and reject anything not related to that belief. In the realm of personal belief I commit myself morally to my convictions and refuse to compromise. But in intimate personal belief I commit myself spiritually to Jesus Christ and make a determination to be dominated by Him alone.

Then, when I stand face to face with Jesus Christ and He says to me, "Do you believe this?" I find that faith is as natural as breathing. And I am staggered when I think how foolish I have been in not trusting Him earlier.

Lord, not with any sense of unworthiness (how can unworthiness indulge in any sense of worthiness?), nor any thought of my insufficiency, nor any thought of myself at all—I come just because You are Yourself.

The Undetected Sacredness
of Circumstances

*"We know that all things work together for good to those who love
God . . . ."* —ROMANS 8:28

The circumstances of a saint's life are ordained of God. In the life of a
saint there is no such thing as chance. God by His providence brings
you into circumstances that you can't understand at all, but the Spirit of
God understands. God brings you to places, among people, and into certain conditions to accomplish a definite purpose through the intercession
of the Spirit in you. Never put yourself in front of your circumstances and
say, "I'm going to be my own providence here; I will watch this closely, or
protect myself from that." All your circumstances are in the hand of God,
and therefore you don't ever have to think they are unnatural or unique.
Your part in intercessory prayer is not to agonize over how to intercede, but
to use the everyday circumstances and people God puts around you by His
providence to bring them before His throne, and to allow the Spirit in you
the opportunity to intercede for them. In this way God is going to touch
the whole world with His saints.

Am I making the Holy Spirit's work difficult by being vague and
unsure, or by trying to do His work for Him? I must do the human side of
intercession—utilizing the circumstances in which I find myself and the
people who surround me. I must keep my conscious life as a sacred place
for the Holy Spirit. Then as I lift different ones to God through prayer, the
Holy Spirit intercedes for them.

Your intercessions can never be mine, and my intercessions can never be
yours, ". . . but the Spirit Himself makes intercession" in each of our lives
(Romans 8:26). And without that intercession, the lives of others would be
left in poverty and in ruin.

---

*Unto You, Lord, do I turn, and on the ground of Your mighty redemption I
pray great triumphing prayers with boldness, knowing that if I ask anything
according to Your will, You hear me.*

⟐ DAY 74 ⟐
The Unrivaled Power of Prayer

"We do not know what we should pray for as we ought, but the Spirit Himself makes intercession for us with groanings which cannot be uttered."
—ROMANS 8:26

We realize that we are energized by the Holy Spirit for prayer; and we know what it is to pray in accordance with the Spirit; but we don't often realize that the Holy Spirit Himself prays prayers in us which we cannot utter ourselves. When we are born again of God and are indwelt by the Spirit of God, He expresses for us the unutterable.

"He," the Holy Spirit in you, "makes intercession for the saints according to the will of God" (8:27). And God searches your heart, not to know what your conscious prayers are, but to find out what the prayer of the Holy Spirit is.

The Spirit of God uses the nature of the believer as a temple in which to offer His prayers of intercession. ". . . your body is the temple of the Holy Spirit . . ." (1 Corinthians 6:19). When Jesus Christ cleansed the temple, ". . . He would not allow anyone to carry wares through the temple" (Mark 11:16). The Spirit of God will not allow you to use your body for your own convenience. Jesus ruthlessly cast out everyone who bought and sold in the temple, and said, "My house shall be called a house of prayer . . . . But you have made it a 'den of thieves'" (Mark 11:17).

Have we come to realize that our "body is the temple of the Holy Spirit"? If so, we must be careful to keep it undefiled for Him. We have to remember that our conscious life, even though only a small part of our total person, is to be regarded by us as a "temple of the Holy Spirit." He will be responsible for the unconscious part which we don't know, but we must pay careful attention to and guard the conscious part for which we are responsible.

O Lord, I pray for the power of Your Spirit that I may adore You in fuller ways. Keep my spirit brightly infused by Your Holy Spirit that, thus energized, the Lord Jesus and His perfections may be manifested in my mortal flesh.

Sacred Service

"I now rejoice in my sufferings for you, and fill up in my flesh what is lacking in the afflictions of Christ . . . ." —COLOSSIANS 1:24

The Christian worker has to be a sacred "go-between." He must be so closely identified with his Lord and the reality of His redemption that Christ can continually bring His creating life through him. I am not referring to the strength of one individual's personality being superimposed on another, but the real presence of Christ coming through every aspect of the worker's life. When we preach the historical facts of the life and death of our Lord as they are conveyed in the New Testament, our words are made sacred. God uses these words, on the basis of His redemption, to create something in those who listen which otherwise could never have been created. If we simply preach the effects of redemption in the human life instead of the revealed, divine truth regarding Jesus Himself, the result is not new birth in those who listen. The result is a refined religious lifestyle, and the Spirit of God cannot witness to it because such preaching is in a realm other than His. We must make sure that we are living in such harmony with God that as we proclaim His truth He can create in others those things which He alone can do.

When we say, "What a wonderful personality, what a fascinating person, and what wonderful insight!" then what opportunity does the gospel of God have through all of that? It cannot get through, because the attraction is to the messenger and not the message. If a person attracts through his personality, that becomes his appeal. If, however, he is identified with the Lord Himself, then the appeal becomes what Jesus Christ can do. The danger is to glory in men, yet Jesus says we are to lift up only *Him* (see John 12:32).

O Lord, in might and majesty prevail in many more ways today. Keep me from secularization of soul or spirit.

⌒ DAY 76 ⌒

Fellowship in the Gospel

". . . fellow laborer in the gospel of Christ . . . ."
—1 THESSALONIANS 3:2

After sanctification, it is difficult to state what your purpose in life is, because God has moved you into His purpose through the Holy Spirit. He is using you now for His purposes throughout the world as He used His Son for the purpose of our salvation. If you seek great things for yourself, thinking, "God has called me for this and for that," you barricade God from using you. As long as you maintain your own personal interests and ambitions, you cannot be completely aligned or identified with God's interests. This can only be accomplished by giving up all of your personal plans once and for all, and by allowing God to take you directly into His purpose for the world. Your understanding of your ways must also be surrendered, because they are now the ways of the Lord.

I must learn that the purpose of my life belongs to God, not me. God is using me from His great personal perspective, and all He asks of me is that I trust Him. I should never say, "Lord, this causes me such heartache." To talk that way makes me a stumbling block. When I stop telling God what I want, He can freely work His will in me without any hindrance. He can crush me, exalt me, or do anything else He chooses. He simply asks me to have absolute faith in Him and His goodness. Self-pity is of the devil, and if I wallow in it I cannot be used by God for His purpose in the world. Doing this creates for me my own cozy "world within the world," and God will not be allowed to move me from it because of my fear of being "frostbitten."

Speak, Lord, that I may hear and understand. There seems so much outwardness in my spiritual life, so little gracious power realized. Quicken me until I am incandescent with You.

⌐ DAY 77 ⌐

The Supreme Climb

"He said, 'Take now your son . . . .'" —GENESIS 22:2

God's command is, "Take *now*," not later. It is incredible how we debate! We know something is right, but we try to find excuses for not doing it immediately. If we are to climb to the height God reveals, it can never be done later—it must be done now. And the sacrifice must be worked through our will before we actually perform it.

"So Abraham rose early in the morning . . . and went to the place of which God had told him" (22:3). Oh, the wonderful simplicity of Abraham! When God spoke, he did not "confer with flesh and blood" (Galatians 1:16). Beware when you want to "confer with flesh and blood" or even your own thoughts, insights, or understandings—anything that is not based on your personal relationship with God. These are all things that compete with and hinder obedience to God.

Abraham did not choose what the sacrifice would be. Always guard against self-chosen service for God. Self-sacrifice may be a disease that impairs your service. If God has made your cup sweet, drink it with grace; or even if He has made it bitter, drink it in communion with Him. If the providential will of God means a hard and difficult time for you, go through it. But never decide the place of your own martyrdom, as if to say, "I will only go to there, but no farther." God chose the test for Abraham, and Abraham neither delayed nor protested, but steadily obeyed. If you are not living in touch with God, it is easy to blame Him or pass judgment on Him. You must go through the trial before you have any right to pronounce a verdict, because by going through the trial you learn to know God better. God is working in us to reach His highest goals until His purpose and our purpose become one.

O Lord, draw near, press into my conscious possession until I am all taken up with You. Make this day radiant with Your power.

The Changed Life

"If anyone is in Christ, he is a new creation; old things have passed away; behold, all things have become new." —2 CORINTHIANS 5:17

What understanding do you have of the salvation of your soul? The work of salvation means that in your real life things are dramatically changed. You no longer look at things in the same way. Your desires are new and the old things have lost their power to attract you. One of the tests for determining if the work of salvation in your life is genuine is—has God changed the things that really matter to you? If you still yearn for the old things, it is absurd to talk about being born from above—you are deceiving yourself. If you are born again, the Spirit of God makes the change very evident in your real life and thought. And when a crisis comes, you are the most amazed person on earth at the wonderful difference there is in you. There is no possibility of imagining that *you* did it. It is this complete and amazing change that is the very evidence that you are saved.

What difference has my salvation and sanctification made? For instance, can I stand in the light of 1 Corinthians 13, or do I squirm and evade the issue? True salvation, worked out in me by the Holy Spirit, frees me completely. And as long as I "walk in the light as He is in the light" (1 John 1:7), God sees nothing to rebuke because His life is working itself into every detailed part of my being, not on the conscious level, but even deeper than my consciousness.

Lord, Your goodness is so beyond comparison that we are "like unto them that dream, our mouth is filled with laughter, and our tongue with singing." We praise You for the time when we shall come again with joy, bringing our sheaves with us.

⌒ DAY 79 ⌒

Faith or Experience?

". . . the Son of God, who loved me and gave Himself for me."
—GALATIANS 2:20

We should battle through our moods, feelings, and emotions into absolute devotion to the Lord Jesus. We must break out of our own little world of experience into abandoned devotion to Him. Think who the New Testament says Jesus Christ is, and then think of the despicable meagerness of the miserable faith we exhibit by saying, "I haven't had this experience or that experience"! Think what faith in Jesus Christ claims and provides—He can present us faultless before the throne of God, inexpressibly pure, absolutely righteous, and profoundly justified. Stand in absolute adoring faith "in Christ Jesus, who became for us wisdom from God—and righteousness and sanctification and redemption . . ." (1 Corinthians 1:30). How dare we talk of making a sacrifice for the Son of God! We are saved from hell and total destruction, and then we talk about making sacrifices!

We must continually focus and firmly place our faith in Jesus Christ—not a "prayer meeting" Jesus Christ, or a "book" Jesus Christ, but the New Testament Jesus Christ, who is God Incarnate, and who ought to strike us dead at His feet. Our faith must be in the One from whom our salvation springs. Jesus Christ wants our absolute, unrestrained devotion to Himself. We can never *experience* Jesus Christ, or selfishly bind Him in the confines of our own hearts. Our faith must be built on strong determined confidence in Him.

It is because of our trusting in experience that we see the steadfast impatience of the Holy Spirit against unbelief. All of our fears are sinful, and we create our own fears by refusing to nourish ourselves in our faith. How can anyone who is identified with Jesus Christ suffer from doubt or fear! Our lives should be an absolute hymn of praise resulting from perfect, irrepressible, triumphant belief.

Lord, be such a reviving and refreshing Presence in our midst today that we can only rejoice as fresh hopes of Eternity walking the actual ways of Time open before our eyes.

∾ DAY 80 ∾
Discovering Divine Design

"As for me, being on the way, the Lord led me . . . ."
—GENESIS 24:27

We should be so one with God that we don't need to ask continually for guidance. Sanctification means that we are made the children of God. A child's life is normally obedient, until he chooses disobedience. But as soon as he chooses to disobey, an inherent inner conflict is produced. On the spiritual level, inner conflict is the warning of the Spirit of God. When He warns us in this way, we must stop at once and be renewed in the spirit of our mind to discern God's will (see Romans 12:2). If we are born again by the Spirit of God, our devotion to Him is hindered, or even stopped, by continually asking Him to guide us here and there. ". . . the Lord led me . . ." and on looking back we see the presence of an amazing design. If we are born of God we will see His guiding hand and give Him the credit.

We can all see God in exceptional things, but it requires the growth of spiritual discipline to see God in every detail. Never believe that the so-called random events of life are anything less than God's appointed order. Be ready to discover His divine designs anywhere and everywhere.

Beware of being obsessed with consistency to your own convictions instead of being devoted to God. If you are a saint and say, "I will never do this or that," in all probability this will be exactly what God will require of you. There was never a more inconsistent being on this earth than our Lord, but He was never inconsistent with His Father. The important consistency in a saint is not to a principle but to the divine life. It is the divine life that continually makes more and more discoveries about the divine mind. It is easier to be an excessive fanatic than it is to be consistently faithful, because God causes an amazing humbling of our religious conceit when we are faithful to Him.

Lord, I look to You for this day. Cause the abundance of Your bounty and beauty to be upon me.

"What Is That to You?"

"Peter . . . said to Jesus, 'But Lord, what about this man?' Jesus said to him, '. . . what is that to you? You follow Me.'" —JOHN 21:21–22

One of the hardest lessons to learn comes from our stubborn refusal to refrain from interfering in other people's lives. It takes a long time to realize the danger of being an amateur providence, that is, interfering with God's plan for others. You see someone suffering and say, "He will not suffer, and I will make sure that he doesn't." You put your hand right in front of God's permissive will to stop it, and then God says, "What is that to you?" Is there stagnation in your spiritual life? Don't allow it to continue, but get into God's presence and find out the reason for it. You will possibly find it is because you have been interfering in the life of another—proposing things you had no right to propose, or advising when you had no right to advise. When you do have to give advice to another person, God will advise through you with the direct understanding of His Spirit. Your part is to maintain the right relationship with God so that His discernment can come through you continually for the purpose of blessing someone else.

Most of us live only within the level of consciousness—consciously serving and consciously devoted to God. This shows immaturity and the fact that we're not yet living the real Christian life. Maturity is produced in the life of a child of God on the unconscious level, until we become so totally surrendered to God that we are not even aware of being used by Him. When we are consciously aware of being used as broken bread and poured-out wine, we have yet another level to reach—a level where all awareness of ourselves and of what God is doing through us is completely eliminated. A saint is never consciously a saint—a saint is consciously dependent on God.

Oh, by Your indwelling Spirit knit me together into worship and beauty and holiness. Lord, touch my body and spirit till both are sweeping in one for You.

❧ DAY 82 ❧

Still Human!

". . . whatever you do, do all to the glory of God."
—1 CORINTHIANS 10:31

In the Scriptures, the great miracle of the incarnation slips into the ordinary life of a child; the great miracle of the transfiguration fades into the demon-possessed valley below; the glory of the resurrection descends into a breakfast on the seashore. This is not an anticlimax, but a great revelation of God.

We have a tendency to look for wonder in our experience, and we mistake heroic actions for real heroes. It's one thing to go through a crisis grandly, yet quite another to go through every day glorifying God when there is no witness, no limelight, and no one paying even the remotest attention to us. If we are not looking for halos, we at least want something that will make people say, "What a wonderful man of prayer he is!" or, "What a great woman of devotion she is!" If you are properly devoted to the Lord Jesus, you have reached the lofty height where no one would ever notice you personally. All that is noticed is the power of God coming through you all the time.

We want to be able to say, "Oh, I have had a wonderful call from God!" But to do even the most humbling tasks to the glory of God takes the Almighty God Incarnate working in us. To be utterly unnoticeable requires God's Spirit in us making us absolutely humanly His. The true test of a saint's life is not successfulness but faithfulness on the human level of life. We tend to set up success in Christian work as our purpose, but our purpose should be to display the glory of God in human life, to live a life "hidden with Christ in God" in our everyday human conditions (Colossians 3:3). Our human relationships are the very conditions in which the ideal life of God should be exhibited.

Lord, how helpless I am in bringing forth fruit, Your kind of fruit in the world, so ungenerous and unlike You am I. Forgive me, and by abiding in Jesus may I bear much fruit and so glorify the Father.

☞ DAY 83 ☜

The Eternal Goal

"By Myself I have sworn, says the Lord, because you have done this thing . . . I will bless you . . . ." —GENESIS 22:16–17

Abraham, at this point, has reached the place where he is in touch with the very nature of God. He now understands the reality of God.

My goal is God Himself . . .
At any cost, dear Lord, by any road.

"At any cost . . . by any road" means submitting to God's way of bringing us to the goal. There is no possibility of questioning God when He speaks, if He speaks to His own nature in me. Prompt obedience is the only result. When Jesus says, "Come," I simply come; when He says, "Let go," I let go; when He says, "Trust God in this matter," I trust. This work of obedience is the evidence that the nature of God is in me.

God's revelation of Himself to me is influenced by my character, not by God's character.

'Tis because I am ordinary,
Thy ways so often look ordinary to me.

It is through the discipline of obedience that I get to the place where Abraham was and I see who God is. God will never be real to me until I come face to face with Him in Jesus Christ. Then I will know and can boldly proclaim, "In all the world, my God, there is none but Thee, there is none but Thee."

The promises of God are of no value to us until, through obedience, we come to understand the nature of God. We may read some things in the Bible every day for a year and they may mean nothing to us. Then, because we have been obedient to God in some small detail, we suddenly see what God means and His nature is instantly opened up to us. "All the promises of God in Him are Yes, and in Him Amen . . ." (2 Corinthians 1:20). Our "Yes" must be born of obedience; when by obedience we ratify a promise of God by saying, "Amen," or, "So be it." That promise becomes ours.

O Lord, rouse and quicken me so that my mortal flesh may indeed be the obedient servant of Your Spirit.

Winning into Freedom

"If the Son makes you free, you shall be free indeed." —JOHN 8:36

If there is even a trace of individual self-satisfaction left in us, it always says, "I can't surrender," or "I can't be free." But the spiritual part of our being never says "I can't"; it simply soaks up everything around it. Our spirit hungers for more and more. It is the way we are built. We are designed with a great capacity for God, but sin, our own individuality, and wrong thinking keep us from getting to Him. God delivers us from sin—we have to deliver ourselves from our individuality. This means offering our natural life to God and sacrificing it to Him, so He may transform it into spiritual life through our obedience.

God pays no attention to our natural individuality in the development of our spiritual life. His plan runs right through our natural life. We must see to it that we aid and assist God, and not stand against Him by saying, "I can't do that." God will not discipline us; we must discipline ourselves. God will not bring our "arguments . . . and every thought into captivity to the obedience of Christ" (2 Corinthians 10:5)—we have to do it. Don't say, "Oh, Lord, I suffer from wandering thoughts." *Don't* suffer from wandering thoughts. Stop listening to the tyranny of your individual natural life and win freedom into the spiritual life.

"If the Son makes you free . . . ." Do not substitute *Savior* for *Son* in this passage. The *Savior* has set us free from sin, but this is the freedom that comes from being set free from myself *by the Son*. It is what Paul meant in Galatians 2:20 when he said, "I have been crucified with Christ . . . ." His individuality had been broken and his spirit had been united with his Lord; not just merged into Him, but made one with Him. ". . . you shall be free indeed"—free to the very core of your being; free from the inside to the outside. We tend to rely on our own energy, instead of being energized by the power that comes from identification with Jesus.

Lord, how completely I need You. And as Your life fills up the limits of my mind and spirit and overflows, glory will be to Your name.

His Birth and Our New Birth

" 'Behold, the virgin shall be with child, and bear a Son, and they shall call His name Immanuel,' which is translated, 'God with us.'"
—MATTHEW 1:23

His Birth in History. ". . . that Holy One who is to be born will be called the Son of God (Luke 1:35). Jesus Christ was born *into* this world, not *from* it. He did not emerge out of history; He came into history from the outside. Jesus Christ is not the best human being the human race can boast of—He is a Being for whom the human race can take no credit at all. He is not man becoming God, but God Incarnate—God coming into human flesh from outside it. His life is the highest and the holiest entering through the most humble of doors. Our Lord's birth was an advent—the appearance of God in human form.

His Birth in Me. "My little children, for whom I labor in birth again until Christ is formed in you . . ." (Galatians 4:19). Just as our Lord came into human history from outside it, He must also come into me from outside. Have I allowed my personal human life to become a "Bethlehem" for the Son of God? I cannot enter the realm of the kingdom of God unless I am born again from above by a birth totally unlike physical birth. "You must be born again" (John 3:7). This is not a command, but a fact based on the authority of God. The evidence of the new birth is that I yield myself so completely to God that "Christ is formed" in me. And once "Christ is formed" in me, His nature immediately begins to work through me.

God Evident in the Flesh. This is what is made so profoundly possible for you and for me through the redemption of man by Jesus Christ.

O Lord, I do praise You that by Your divine omnipotent grace I am learning to come into Your presence. Touch my body and spirit with Your grace and light and wisdom. Raise me to the level of such glorious service that I may catch Your likeness.

Where the Battle Is Won or Lost

" 'If you will return, O Israel,' says the Lord . . . ." —JEREMIAH 4:1

O ur battles are first won or lost in the secret places of our will in God's presence, never in full view of the world. The Spirit of God seizes me and I am compelled to get alone with God and fight the battle before Him. Until I do this, I will lose every time. The battle may take one minute or one year, but that will depend on me, not God. However long it takes, I must wrestle with it alone before God, and I must resolve to go through the hell of renunciation or rejection before Him. Nothing has any power over someone who has fought the battle before God and won there.

I should never say, "I will wait until I get into difficult circumstances and then I'll put God to the test." Trying to do that will not work. I must first get the issue settled between God and myself in the secret places of my soul, where no one else can interfere. Then I can go ahead, knowing with certainty that the battle is won. Lose it there, and calamity, disaster, and defeat before the world are as sure as the laws of God. The reason the battle is lost is that I fight it first in the external world. Get alone with God, do battle before Him, and settle the matter once and for all.

In dealing with other people, our stance should always be to drive them toward making a decision of their will. That is how surrendering to God begins. Not often, but every once in a while, God brings us to a major turning point—a great crossroads in our life. From that point we either go toward a more and more slow, lazy, and useless Christian life, or we become more and more on fire, giving our utmost for *His* highest—our best for *His* glory.

It is time, O my God, for a touch from You, one of those great transfiguring touches in which You stand out plainly and clearly from all else—brilliant moments in which I see You and worship and wonder.

⮚ DAY 87 ⮘

Continuous Conversion

". . . unless you are converted and become as little children, you will by
no means enter the kingdom of heaven." —MATTHEW 18:3

These words of our Lord refer to our initial conversion, but we should continue to turn to God as children, being continuously converted every day of our lives. If we trust in our own abilities, instead of God's, we produce consequences for which God will hold us responsible. When God through His sovereignty brings us into new situations, we should immediately make sure that our natural life submits to the spiritual, obeying the orders of the Spirit of God. Just because we have responded properly in the past is no guarantee that we will do so again. The response of the natural to the spiritual should be continuous conversion, but this is where we so often refuse to be obedient. No matter what our situation is, the Spirit of God remains unchanged and His salvation unaltered. But we must "put on the new man . . ." (Ephesians 4:24). God holds us accountable every time we refuse to convert ourselves, and He sees our refusal as willful disobedience. Our natural life must not rule—God must rule in us.

To refuse to be continuously converted puts a stumbling block in the growth of our spiritual life. There are areas of self-will in our lives where our pride pours contempt on the throne of God and says, "I won't submit." We deify our independence and self-will and call them by the wrong name. What God sees as stubborn weakness, we call strength. There are whole areas of our lives that have not yet been brought into submission, and this can only be done by this continuous conversion. Slowly but surely we can claim the whole territory for the Spirit of God.

O Lord, that I might be brought into Your presence and see things from Your
standpoint. Anoint me afresh today, O Lord, with Your gracious Spirit.

❧ DAY 88 ❧

Deserter or Disciple?

"From that time many of His disciples went back and walked with Him no more." —JOHN 6:66

When God, by His Spirit through His Word, gives you a clear vision of His will, you must "walk in the light" of that vision (1 John 1:7). Even though your mind and soul may be thrilled by it, if you don't "walk in the light" of it you will sink to a level of bondage never envisioned by our Lord. Mentally disobeying the "heavenly vision" (Acts 26:19) will make you a slave to ideas and views that are completely foreign to Jesus Christ. Don't look at someone else and say, "Well, if he can have those views and prosper, why can't I?" You have to "walk in the light" of the vision that has been given to *you.* Don't compare yourself with others or judge them— that is between God and them. When you find that one of your favorite and strongly held views clashes with the "heavenly vision," do not begin to debate it. If you do, a sense of property and personal right will emerge in you—things on which Jesus placed no value. He was against these things as being the root of everything foreign to Himself—". . . for one's life does not consist in the abundance of the things he possesses" (Luke 12:15). If we don't see and understand this, it is because we are ignoring the underlying principles of our Lord's teaching.

Our tendency is to lie back and bask in the memory of the wonderful experience we had when God revealed His will to us. But if a New Testament standard is revealed to us by the light of God, and we don't try to measure up, or even feel inclined to do so, then we begin to backslide. It means your conscience does not respond to the truth. You can never be the same after the unveiling of a truth. That moment marks you as one who either continues on with even more devotion as a disciple of Jesus Christ, or as one who turns to go back as a deserter.

Lord, fill every space around me with Yourself this day. Control everything right marvelously by Your guiding hand. Lift me up into Your wonderful purposes, and keep me from impulsiveness.

"And Every Virtue We Possess"

". . . All my springs are in you." —PSALM 87:7

Our Lord never "patches up" our natural virtues, that is, our natural traits, qualities, or characteristics. He completely remakes a person on the inside—". . . put on the new man . . ." (Ephesians 4:24). In other words, see that your natural human life is putting on all that is in keeping with the new life. The life God places within us develops its own new virtues, not the virtues of the seed of Adam, but of Jesus Christ. Once God has begun the process of sanctification in your life, watch and see how God causes your confidence in your own natural virtues and power to wither away. He will continue until you learn to draw your life from the reservoir of the resurrection life of Jesus. Thank God if you are going through this drying-up experience!

The sign that God is at work in us is that He is destroying our confidence in the natural virtues, because they are not promises of what we are going to be, but only a wasted reminder of what God created man to be. We want to cling to our natural virtues, while all the time God is trying to get us in contact with the life of Jesus Christ—a life that can never be described in terms of natural virtues. It is the saddest thing to see people who are trying to serve God depending on that which the grace of God never gave them. They are depending solely on what they have by virtue of heredity. God does not take our natural virtues and transform them, because our natural virtues could never even come close to what Jesus Christ wants. No natural love, no natural patience, no natural purity can ever come up to His demands. But as we bring every part of our natural bodily life into harmony with the new life God has placed within us, He will exhibit in us the virtues that were characteristic of the Lord Jesus.

And every virtue we possess
Is His alone.

O Lord, all my fresh springs are in You. To You I come; may Your mighty life spring up in me, a veritable influx into body as well as spirit.

❧ DAY 90 ❧

Yesterday

"You shall not go out with haste, . . . for the Lord will go before you, and the God of Israel will be your rear guard." —ISAIAH 52:12

Security from Yesterday. ". . . God requires an account of what is past" (Ecclesiastes 3:15). At the end of the year we turn with eagerness to all that God has for the future, and yet anxiety is apt to arise when we remember our yesterdays. Our present enjoyment of God's grace tends to be lessened by the memory of yesterday's sins and blunders. But God is the God of our yesterdays, and He allows the memory of them to turn the past into a ministry of spiritual growth for our future. God reminds us of the past to protect us from a very shallow security in the present.

Security for Tomorrow. ". . . the Lord will go before you . . . ." This is a gracious revelation—that God will send His forces out where we have failed to do so. He will keep watch so that we will not be tripped up again by the same failures, as would undoubtedly happen if He were not our "rear guard." And God's hand reaches back to the past, settling all the claims against our conscience.

Security for Today. "You shall not go out with haste . . . ." As we go forth into the coming year, let it not be in the haste of impetuous, forgetful delight, nor with the quickness of impulsive thoughtlessness. But let us go out with the patient power of knowing that the God of Israel will go before us. Our yesterdays hold broken and irreversible things for us. It is true that we have lost opportunities that will never return, but God can transform this destructive anxiety into a constructive thoughtfulness for the future. Let the past rest, but let it rest in the sweet embrace of Christ.

Leave the broken, irreversible past in His hands, and step out into the invincible future with Him.

Lord Jesus, in You "dwells all the fullness of the Godhead," and all power has been given to You "in heaven and on earth." O God, my heavenly Father, supply my every need according to Your riches in glory in Christ Jesus.

⌁ SCRIPTURE INDEX ⌁

17:21 . . . . .Day 47
20:28 . . . . .Day 4
21:17 . . . . .Day 19, 20, 21
21:21–22 . . . . .Day 81

Acts
20:24 . . . . .Day 22, 23
24:16 . . . . .Day 38
26:16 . . . . .Day 10
26:19 . . . . .Day 29

Romans
6:16 . . . . .Day 32
8:26 . . . . .Day 74
8:28 . . . . .Day 73
8:35 . . . . .Day 44
8:37 . . . . .Day 25

1 Corinthians
6:19 . . . . .Day 67
10:31 . . . . .Day 82

2 Corinthians
3:18 . . . . .Day 9
4:10 . . . . .Day 39
5:14 . . . . .Day 14
5:17 . . . . .Day 78
6:1 . . . . .Day 62
6:4 . . . . .Day 24

Galatians
1:15 . . . . .Day 11
1:15–16 . . . . .Day 3
2:20 . . . . .Day 26, 69, 79

Ephesians
1:18 . . . . .Day 40

Philippians
1:20 . . . . .Day 1
2:12–13 . . . . . .Day 51
3:12 . . . . .Day 64

Colossians
1:24 . . . . .Day 75

1 Thessalonians
3:2 . . . . .Day 76

2 Timothy
4:2 . . . . .Day 28

Hebrews
11:8 . . . . .Day 33
13:5 . . . . .Day 49
13:5–6 . . . . . .Day 50

James
4:8 . . . . .Day 70

1 Peter
4:13 . . . . .Day 71

2 Peter
1:4 . . . . .Day 41
1:5 . . . . .Day 35, 60
1:5, 7 . . . . . . .Day 36
1:8 . . . . .Day 37

NOTES

NOTES

NOTES

ᴖ NOTES ᴖ

NOTES

~ NOTES ~

NOTES

NOTES

❧ NOTES ❧

⌒ NOTE TO THE READER ⌒

The publisher invites you to share your response to the message of this book by writing Discovery House, P.O. Box 3566, Grand Rapids, MI 49501, U.S.A. For information about other Discovery House books, music, videos, or DVDs, contact us at the same address or call 1-800-653-8333. Find us at dhp.org or send e-mail to books@dhp.org.